CW01086719

What Every AI
Should Know

What Every Alcoholic Should Know

Cyril F. Kilb, PhD

Edited by Jenny Sidri

iUniverse, Inc.
New York Lincoln Shanghai

What Every Alcoholic Should Know

Copyright © 2006 by Jenny Sidri

All rights reserved. No part of this book may be used or reproduced by any means, graphic, electronic, or mechanical, including photocopying, recording, taping or by any information storage retrieval system without the written permission of the publisher except in the case of brief quotations embodied in critical articles and reviews.

iUniverse books may be ordered through booksellers or by contacting:

iUniverse
2021 Pine Lake Road, Suite 100
Lincoln, NE 68512
www.iuniverse.com
1-800-Authors (1-800-288-4677)

ISBN-13: 978-0-595-36095-6 (pbk)
ISBN-13: 978-0-595-80541-9 (ebk)
ISBN-10: 0-595-36095-5 (pbk)
ISBN-10: 0-595-80541-8 (ebk)

Printed in the United States of America

Contents

Foreword

The author of this book was Dr. Cyril Kilb, my uncle, who guided me. From him, I learned truths about psychology, human relationships, and self-understanding.

Following my uncle's death in 2003, I discovered the Upper Fraternity lessons he had created nearly fifty years earlier to help recovering alcoholics. The lessons were devised as a follow-up to the Alcoholics Anonymous (AA) Twelve Step Program. Members who joined the Upper Fraternity had a few years of sobriety behind them and found help in this self-therapy program.

Dr. Kilb had intended to publish the lessons in a book. It is my privilege to offer his book to those seeking true sobriety.

J. Sidri

Introduction

This book had its start in 1957 as a series of free lessons titled "The Upper Fraternity." These lessons offered a method for alcoholics to improve their self-understanding and make a quicker return to true sobriety. The lessons were sent by request to alcoholics who were advanced in the AA program.

The Upper Fraternity was not affiliated with AA or the Alcoholics Anonymous Foundation, nor was the Fraternity at variance with the teachings of AA. Rather, the Fraternity added to the basic truths of the Twelve Steps, using science and psychology to prove that the Twelve Steps offer us the only right way to live.

Pleasant thoughts and pleasant emotions produce health and happiness. But recovering alcoholics understand the anxiety that negative experiences deposit in their minds. Until an alcoholic learns how to control his own mind, he can never obtain health, happiness, and success.

Self-therapy follows group therapy. AA offers group therapy. This book will guide you through self-therapy with lessons and exercises that aim to rebuild the body and the mind. In developing these lessons, the author sought ways for individuals to relieve everyday tensions and find true relaxation. For over seven years, he attended lectures and talked to hundreds of alcoholics, priests, ministers, rabbis, psychiatrists, psychoanalysts, and psychologists. He attended more than one thousand AA meetings and studied hypnotism and other autosuggestion therapies. He also kept a daily diary and completed an honest self-analysis. Using these techniques, he evolved a system of self-therapy for alcoholics who are past the "first drink" stage.

This system is an extension of all that AA stands for. It does not discuss religion, but like AA, advocates the acceptance of some divine source in which to bathe the ailing mind and develop reverence for a Higher Power. As does AA, this system puts the responsibility for spiritual awakening on the individual.

These lessons offer alcoholics a way to find physical and mental repose and a renewed sense of optimism and self-control. Properly applied, these lessons will bring the "dry" alcoholic health, happiness, and success.

Lesson 1
Positive Thinking and Pleasant Emotions

John stumbled through the front door; he was drunk again. Mary, his wife, was in bed by this time. John found the bottle of liquor hidden in the wood bin and flopped on the couch for another drink: one more swig before heading to bed.

For any alcoholic, this is a familiar scene. How did John become this way? His past brought him to this state.

In Alcoholics Anonymous, we discuss drinking. In this book, we discuss thinking. Why? In order to stop drinking, we have to change our alcoholic thinking. Our first step is to learn the relationship between thinking and drinking.

Experts on alcoholism disagree about its causes. Some claim alcoholism is caused by faulty glands or a vitamin deficiency. Still others assert it is a mental or emotional disease. But they all agree that alcoholism is a psychosomatic illness involving a compulsion to drink and emotional disturbance.

We in AA are experts in our own way because we have suffered this disease and are recovering from it. We know, for example, that our compulsion to drink was driven by negative thinking. We also know that we achieved sobriety only after joining AA and learning to think positively. In our example above, John stumbled drunkenly through the front door as a result of his continued negative thinking. We realize his negative thinking increased his drinking tendency, whereas positive thinking would have paved his way to sobriety.

Negative thinking brings more drinking.

Positive thinking ends the drinking.

There is a cause-and-effect relationship between negative thinking and unhappiness. Let us begin with a typical AA story and examine this relationship as it concerns alcoholism.

As a teenager from a poor family, Mary B. felt rejected and ashamed. She felt awkward and unattractive and not accepted by her peers. Her parents tried to help, but even their advice seemed critical. Lost in negative thinking, Mary became a withdrawn, uncommunicative young woman. Silently, in her heart, she hated her parents, the world, herself—everything.

At a graduation gathering when introduced to the "soothing effects of alcohol," Mary clung to drinking as a way to douse the fire of her resentment and fears. Soon, she could not live without alcohol. She existed solely for the bottle and for escaping into the fantasies and hallucinations of alcoholism.

Finally, after years of drinking, Mary reached the end of the road and sought help at AA. There she poured out her heart to listeners who could empathize with her and accept her. Her feelings of rejection and frustration disappeared. She no longer had to hide her fears, and she felt understood for the first time in her life. Mary embraced the AA program enthusiastically, and her thinking changed from pessimism to optimism; moreover, her resentment was replaced with love for the kindly, understanding AA members around her. She received help to carry her over the trouble spots, and she sobered up with the help of a Higher Power and the Twelve Steps.

What made Mary sober? She changed her alcoholic thinking. When she reached bottom and found herself longing for sobriety, she became determined to change. Now she could be helped because she wanted help. The kindness and understanding of the AA group helped Mary become receptive to positive thinking. Her negative thoughts gave way to positive thoughts of love, kindness, and truth. Before, Mary had closed herself off from everyone. But in the company of positive-thinking AA members, her attitude changed, and her confidence returned. Gradually, Mary adjusted to society and learned how to be happy, healthy, and successful.

When Mary became sober and began to take inventory of her emotions, she discovered that having negative feelings caused her to close up. But positive emotions brought the opposite reaction; they made her feel free, wonderfully at ease, and in good humor. She felt this pattern again and again. Finally, she became convinced that being negative was the quickest way to slip. Love, kindness, and positive thinking were life; resentment, frustration, and negative thinking were sickness and unhappiness. And she realized years later that this applied to everyone, alcoholic or not. To be really healthy, happy, and successful, people must rid themselves of all unpleasant thinking.

Like Mary, every alcoholic must take a thorough inventory of his emotions. But it is difficult for alcoholics to complete this task while still drinking. In most cases, their inability to face themselves is the reason they drink. Mary realized this almost immediately after she turned away from alcohol. Although each drinking experience is different, the backgrounds of all alcoholics have one thing in common: negative emotions. Mary had stumbled upon the very foundation of psychosomatic medicine.

She began to understand that every thought we think registers upon our mind with a corresponding emotion. Unpleasant thoughts create unpleasant emotions that create tensions and constrictions that adversely affect our glands, nerves, and muscles. This is the basis of all psychosomatic illness.

In psychosomatic illness, the mind affects the body (*psyche* means mind; *soma* means body). Experts tell us that alcoholism is a psychosomatic, or emotionally induced, illness. And with both illnesses, the more intelligent a person is, the more prone he or she is to the disease. Why is this? An alcoholic has an alert mind and a sensitive nature and generally is of better than average intelligence. The alcoholic's alert mind finds more to worry about than the mind that is less alert. The alert mind takes on more responsibilities, has more ambition, and thus experiences more tense emotion. These unpleasant emotions are what cause all emotionally induced illnesses.

Now the questions come. Exactly what is an emotion? How do tense, unpleasant emotions induce illnesses? Psychologist William James defined an emotion as "a state of mind that manifests itself by sensible changes in the body." This means that when we think something, that thought registers somewhere in our body and causes a physical change. If the thought is pleasant, the bodily change is pleasant; if the thought is unpleasant, the bodily change is unpleasant. Since we are constantly thinking, we are constantly creating emotions that must register somewhere in our body as either pleasant or unpleasant changes. Pleasant thinking makes us healthy and happy, and unpleasant thinking makes us ill and unhappy.

Pleasant emotions, such as happiness and joy, come from pleasant thoughts, such as remembering the affection of a child or the joy of a daughter's wedding day. We have all experienced wonderful days when we feel in perfect health and everything is just right. On such days we think, speak, and act in a pleasant manner and are optimistic, confident, happy, healthy, serene, and agreeable. Our wonderful attitude toward life and our relaxed body go hand in hand, for pleasant thoughts cause pleasant feelings. These pleasant feelings put our body in perfect harmony, and we are "on the beam" or "in tune," as the sayings go. Days like these come from pleasant experiences that make us feel wonderful and bring pleasant thoughts. These pleasant thoughts cause proper body functioning; proper body functioning makes us feel good and brings more pleasant thoughts, and the cycle goes on. If all days were so perfect, we would always experience pleasant emotions and enjoy continuous perfect health and absolute happiness.

Unfortunately, however, we all experience unpleasant emotions, too, and these persistent unpleasant emotions overstimulate parts of our body and cause unpleasant feelings that result in illness. Unpleasant emotions such as anger, resentment, hate, anxiety, defeat, grief, dissatisfaction, apprehension, worry, and so on originate from unpleasant thoughts. For example, if we are fearful of losing our job or anxious about money problems or worried about a landlord or tenant, or if we resent the constant criticism of someone or feel anger after being reprimanded by our boss, we experience unpleasant thoughts and emotions. When such negative thoughts persist, the resulting unpleasant emotions, like the relentless drip of water upon a rock, eventually erode the harmonious functioning of our endocrine systems, and the amount of hormones that flow into our blood is out of balance. This imbalance within the bodily system, when prolonged, leads to illness. The severity of the illness will vary with the intensity and type of emotion, the condition of the body and mind, and the length of time the emotion has persisted.

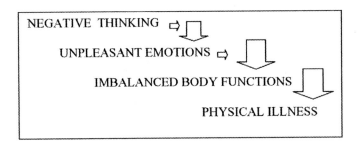

For example, suppose an employee believed his boss became unjustly angry with him. The employee, instead of discussing the problem rationally, brooded and grumbled about the issue. He found himself unable to eat normally anymore, and a doctor finally diagnosed him with an ulcer. This is the path that negative thinking follows. Negative thoughts can produce angry emotions. Continual anger overstimulates the body (causing reddening of the face or constriction of muscles, for instance) and can eventually lead to illness, such as an ulcer or heart attack.

Understanding the relationships among emotions, thinking, and drinking is critical to developing self-understanding. For our health's sake, we must strive constantly to have pleasant emotions. As we say in AA, "This is simple but not easy."

Begin to observe your thinking and guard your thoughts as closely as you would guard your money. When you feel blue or upset, smile anyway, and find something to be grateful for. Do something constructive and creative. Work on being positive, because your health, happiness, and success depend on pleasant thinking.

Lesson 2
Two Kinds of Sobriety

There are two kinds of sobriety: superficial and real. Superficial sobriety occurs when we first stop drinking, join AA, and learn about the Twelve Steps. Real sobriety is complete sobriety, and produces serenity, health, happiness, and prosperity. True sobriety comes in three stages. First we "dry up the stomach" by joining AA. Then we "open the heart" by honestly caring about others and believing we can achieve true sobriety. Finally, we face the toughest job of all, "clearing up the head," or completely straightening out our thinking through self-analysis.

Let's discuss some difficulties that may occur in each stage. Some newcomers to AA never dry up the stomach because they cannot accept the AA program. This generally means that they cannot turn their will over to a Higher Power. They lack the ability to have confidence in anything or anyone. They slip. And behind every slip is a negative state of mind that makes them lose control. This is an important point: to keep ourselves dry in the stomach, we must never lose control. How do we accomplish this? By never letting our negative emotions get control.

When, in anger, we feel ready to yell or slam the door, we learn to control these negative thoughts and emotions. When worry descends heavily, instead of retreating into a shell and sneaking a drink, we learn how to face worries and think of logical ways to overcome obstacles. How? We do this through developing the practice of positive thinking. We all experience frustrations. The point is to learn a new, positive reaction to these frustrations.

On our journey to sobriety, we all feel these negative emotions at times, for some situations are beyond our control. Until we learn how to do away with unpleasant emotions, we must hold them in check. To do this, we must put forth the effort to understand and control our mind. It can be done.

In the Twelve Steps, we are told to turn our will over to a Higher Power, an authority above ourselves. The inability to do this leads to frustration and, finally, to some kind of breakdown. Nobody can be healthy, happy, and successful without some kind of help of someone or something. No one has all the answers. That is why the world has God. As long as there is the unknown, there will always be someone above us in knowledge. The person who cannot take advice or cannot take orders experiences trouble because his mind is closed to all ideas except his own. Those who slip for various psychological reasons are unable to accept anybody else's ideas. In our drinking days, we were all guilty of this lack of reason.

Now that we are not drinking, we must be as rational as possible. This means that we must do two things: (1) not take that first drink; and (2) find out why we were irrational (and began drinking). This brings us to the stage where we must open up the heart.

Life is meant to be a happy experience. We must open up our hearts, believe that happiness is possible, and discipline ourselves to think pleasantly at all times. For example, we look on the bright side and speak optimistically. Instead of lamenting how little time there is to get a chore done, we think cheerfully about how much *can* get done. Instead of whining about the long line we're waiting in, we are grateful to be able to buy anything at all, and we offer words of cheer to those waiting with us. The practice of positive thinking results in good emotions, which help us persevere on the road to true sobriety.

No one can succeed in a task unless she believes in what she is doing. And effort follows thought. Therefore, we must open up the heart—believe—before we can clear up the heart—put forth the effort to understand ourselves. Belief generates thinking, and thinking generates action. Thus, we must open up the heart (believe) before we can clear up the head (think positively and act positively). Anna Pavolova, the famous Russian ballerina, came from a home of poverty, but she believed with all her heart that she could be and would be a ballerina. Little Anna practiced hard for years, and, at the age of ten years she completed for admission to the St. Petersburg Ballet Academy and was accepted. Her belief generated her action. We can do the same: believe we can achieve true sobriety and think positively in order to reach our goal. Constructive action is bound to follow.

STEPS TO TRUE SOBRIETY

1. *DRY UP THE STOMACH*
   a. Stop drinking
   b. Study our irrational thinking

2. *OPEN UP THE HEART*
   a. Believe that health and happiness exist for us now
   b. Care about others

3. *CLEAR UP THE HEAD*
   a. Think and act positively
   b. Do daily self-analysis

Now that we have established the importance of positive thinking, let's look at how unpleasant emotions cause psychosomatic (emotionally induced) illness. This should be enough to make us stop thinking negatively.

Anger, one of the worst unpleasant emotions, can cause great harm to our bodies. Anger causes the blood to clot more quickly. Stomach muscles constrict so tightly that nothing can leave, and the digestive tract becomes spastic. Severe abdominal pain sometimes results. The heart beats faster, and blood pressure rises. If it rises high enough, a person will "blow" a blood vessel and suffer a cerebral hemorrhage. Anger can cause angina pectoris or even a fatal coronary occlusion, the squeezing down of the heart arteries. The death certificates of angry people may read "exhausted heart," "coronary occlusion," or "heart attack."

Anger is only one of many unpleasant emotions that cause emotionally induced illness. If we have aches and pains, gas in the stomach, stiff necks, and constipation, we are showing the effects of unpleasant emotions. Maintaining good emotions is the basis of happiness and constructive action.

Lesson 3
How Unpleasant Emotions Cause Psychosomatic Illness, Part I

Since we are constantly thinking, we are constantly creating emotions, and every emotion registers somewhere in our body. Pleasant emotions energize the body in a balanced way and make us happy and healthy, whereas unpleasant emotions do the opposite. The unpleasant emotion of anger can even lead to death. It's now time to explain how unpleasant emotions can cause psychosomatic illness, while pleasant emotions produce health and happiness.

Whenever we criticize someone, we hurt ourselves, because the criticism and its unpleasant emotion must first register in our own minds. For example, if I resent the lovely, new dress of my neighbor, I am apt to say, in resentment, to a friend, "Did you see Sandra strutting around in that new dress!! She thinks she's so much better than we are!" The emotion of resentment in my mind registered somewhere in my body even before I said the unkind words, and this negative emotion produced a negative response in my body. Moreover, the resentful thought, by itself, can produce the same negative effect on my body. Have you ever noticed the intensity of anger in the voice of someone who is unkindly criticizing another? The negative emotion is negatively affecting the speaker's body, though the speaker may be unaware of this fact. (As an aside, there are times when constructive criticism is necessary, such as a teacher to a student or parent to a child. But whenever there is criticism to be given, the speaker does well to say the words in an objective way, without condemnation.)

Other types of negativism, such as envy, sarcasm, and deceit, produce the same negative effects on our body. Unpleasant thoughts cause unpleasant emotions that, like chickens, "always come home to roost." We cannot be negative to others in thought, word, or deed without first being negative to ourselves. This is scientifically true, although few people realize it.

9

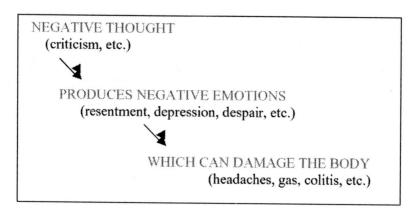

A quick anatomy lesson can show us how thoughts, emotions, and health are related. The human nervous system has two main parts: the central nervous system and the peripheral nervous system. The central nervous system comprises the brain and spinal cord. The peripheral nervous system consists of the nerves that radiate from the brain and spinal cord to outlying parts of the body.

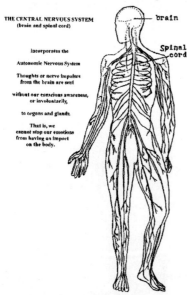

THE CENTRAL NERVOUS SYSTEM
(brain and spinal cord)

Incorporates the

Autonomic Nervous System

Thoughts or nerve impulses from the brain are sent

without our conscious awareness, or involuntarily,

to organs and glands.

That is, we cannot stop our emotions from having an impact on the body.

One part of this peripheral nervous system is called the autonomic nervous system. The autonomic nervous system automatically controls the activities of our organs: our eyes, salivary glands, heart, trachea and bronchi, esophagus, pancreas, stomach, small intestine, first and second part of the large intestine, and bladder. Nerve impulses (generated by our thoughts) are sent from our brain to our autonomic nervous system and from our autonomic nervous system to these organs.

Although we cannot consciously control our autonomic nervous system, its function is affected by our thinking. Every thought begins an automatic cause-and-effect reaction. If the thought is pleasant, the resulting good emotions produce harmonious reactions in the body. Said in another way, good emotions result in the harmonious functioning of the endocrine system in the body. For example, when a tiny child sees a returning parent, the child is happy, and the body functions harmoniously. On the other hand, unpleasant thoughts trigger negative emotions that tear down the body. For example, when we suffer from nervous tension (such as stress or anxiety), it is probably due to muscle-tensing emotions that have continued for a long period.

When we feel a pain in the neck or a lump in the throat, chances are we are suffering from emotional tightness in our neck or throat muscles. When we say this or that "gives me a pain in the neck," we are literally talking our autonomic nervous system into registering pains in our neck. Statistics show that most patients who complain to doctors about neck pain are found to have an emotional tightness of muscles at the upper part of the esophagus. This tightness feels like a lump.

When our stomach muscles tighten because of various unpleasant emotions, we may feel a lump in the upper part of our abdomen. We might even think we have a "stone" there or perhaps an ulcer. Fifty percent of patients who think they have ulcers are actually suffering from emotional muscle pain in the stomach. The colon, which responds to emotions more than any other organ, has been referred to through the ages as the "mirror of the mind." Some people get neck pain, and others get spasms of the colon. Half of the people with troubled colons incorrectly call these pains "gallbladder attacks," while others believe they have gallstones.

This list shows the prevalence of some common emotionally induced illnesses that doctors treat:

Gas and gas pains 95%	Pain in the back of neck 75%
Dizziness 80%	Constipation 70%
Lump in the throat 90%	Ulcer-like pain 50%
Tiredness 90%	Gallbladder-like pain 50%

Current statistics reinforce these percentages. Recent information shows that 87 percent of all emotionally based illnesses manifest with medical symptoms.

Other psychosomatic illnesses include emotional appendicitis, bloating, migraine headaches, tight muscles, bursitis, rheumatism, and neurodermatitis (emotionally induced skin trouble). These illnesses are quite real, and no one can deny that they cause aches and pains. They arise from unpleasant emotions that overstimulate the autonomic nervous system and cause constriction of certain muscles, organs, and nerves. If we can stop the negative thinking behind unpleasant emotions, we can remove the cause of our psychosomatic aches and pains. This is the only road to real sobriety, the state of health, happiness, and success.

There are few alcoholics who are entirely free from emotionally induced aches and pains when they first join AA. This is because they still suffer from stress and strain and have not yet changed their negative thinking. A newcomer becomes a successful old-timer only when he changes his thinking enough to stop drinking and to face life with a pleasant attitude. But if he becomes an old-timer and still persists in negative thinking, he will slip, or he will be merely dry in the stomach (that is, only superficially sober), and this is not enough.

We must do more than give up alcohol. We must refuse to live with the same negative thinking we had while drinking. If we do not, we will continue to punish ourselves mentally, as well as physically, and our emotionally induced illness will manifest itself as something besides alcoholism. We became alcoholics because our negative thinking fanned the fires of our self-destruction. We literally burned ourselves out with frustrations, resentments, hatreds, disappointments, failures, jealousies, envy, inferiority, and a host of other unpleasant emotions. When we joined AA, our newfound hope and courage lifted us high enough to temporarily escape the constant unpleasant emotions we had harbored for years. This state is what we call superficial sobriety.

Superficial sobriety is not enough, however, for it will not bring health, happiness, and success. When our pleasant emotions become strong enough, we are ready to continue toward real sobriety. We must leave any "pink cloud" we may still be on and come down to earth to face ourselves. Our progress depends entirely on our attitude. If we are honest with ourselves, and realistic and unselfish, this attitude will bring pleasant emotions that will give us the power to forge ahead. If we are dishonest with ourselves, and are weak, insincere, and still negative toward life, this attitude will bring unpleasant emotions and make us miserable; we will never enjoy health, happiness, or success.

We should know by now that anything that happens to us is the result of our own actions. Our actions are the result of our own thinking. We cannot blame other people or our circumstances for our troubles, past or present. We have learned to be constructively critical of ourselves. We examine our motives to find the real us, instead of blaming others for our troubles. By doing this, we can understand ourselves better and try to rectify our faults and bad habits.

We must discipline ourselves to exclude negative thinking from our daily lives. It is simple but not easy. We are the only ones who can do it because only we know what is going on in our own minds. The sooner we start a program of self-improvement, the sooner we start a better life.

Lesson 4
How Unpleasant Emotions Cause Psychosomatic Illness, Part II

During our drinking days, there were times when we were unable to express our true feelings. Instead of letting our emotions out, we kept them bottled up inside. Remembering that unpleasant emotions cause damage to our mind and body, we now realize what terrible damage we did to ourselves in the past by repressing our feelings. We should be aware that each of us has a breaking point. When we reach this breaking point, it is far healthier to release our negative thoughts, in the most constructive manner possible, than to hold them in. This holding in, or repressing, builds up pressure that must eventually manifest itself in our bodies as psychosomatic illness.

In the past, we all repressed too many of our negative thoughts. We had various reasons for doing this. Some of us lacked confidence in ourselves and could not speak up because we were afraid of our parents, or people, or situations. Some of us were afraid of failure, and others were afraid of criticism. Still others were forced to live in another's shadow, such as one spouse who is dominated by the other spouse, or a child who lives in the shadow of a talented sibling. There are as many reasons for repression as there are individuals, but each alcoholic tries to escape the pain of unhappiness either consciously or unconsciously by drinking. On the outside, she presents a certain personality pattern that often hides her true negative feelings.

Personality, traced back to its Greek origin, means "mask." The alcoholic masks her true emotions by adopting a certain type of personality to adjust to the outside world. Some of us became arrogant know-it-alls, although inside we were very unsure of ourselves. We used alcohol to bolster our waning confidence. Some of us went to the opposite extreme and escaped into shyness, cowardice, overcautiousness, and similar behaviors. Others became psychopathic liars, lying to themselves and sometimes to others. Others went so far astray they became criminals. In thought, word, and deed, we were all extremists.

Whatever personality we adopted while drinking, it was an adjustment to life that did not work. We made this adjustment because it seemed less painful than facing unpleasant situations. Facing such situations required facing ourselves, and we could not do this. So we turned to the fantasies produced by alcohol and thought we were releasing our tensions through drinking. This was not true release, however, because negative emotions remain in our minds until we consciously release them by understanding them.

This brings us to the point we are at today. The amount of self-knowledge we possess today is in proportion to the amount of daily inventory we have been taking since we first attained sobriety. However, none of us can do this job alone. We need help from professional counselors or from alcoholics who have succeeded in self-adjustment by using the scientific technique of self-analysis.

This book describes a method of self-analysis for alcoholics. A thinking person realizes that his drinking must be rooted in an emotional disturbance, and that only he can control himself because what goes on in his mind is his personal problem. We need to study our thoughts, our motives, and search for fears we hold deep inside, for our hidden fears affect our outward actions.

As alcoholics, we could not live life with enthusiasm and proper self-confidence because we were afraid. Fear is the basis of every unpleasant or negative emotion. If we were not afraid, we would not have bottled up our emotions; we would have been able to release them.

The Endocrine Glands

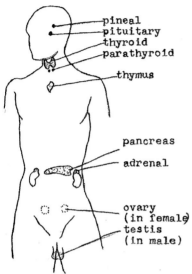

pineal
pituitary
thyroid
parathyroid

thymus

pancreas

adrenal

ovary
(in female)
testis
(in male)

We cannot directly control our autonomic nervous system because it works involuntarily and responds indirectly to our thinking. Pleasant emotions stimulate our autonomic nervous system in a "just right" manner, causing our organs, nerves, and glands to respond harmoniously. This relaxes us and puts us at ease, and leads to good health. Unpleasant emotions do the opposite, overstimulating our autonomic nervous system and ultimately producing tension and disease. Let us apply these concepts to the endocrine system to see how overstimulation of various glands by unpleasant emotions can cause harmful or fatal effects.

Our endocrine glands are called ductless glands because they secrete their hormones directly into the bloodstream. They consist of the pituitary and pineal glands, situated in the cavity of our skull; the thyroid and parathyroids, located near the larynx at the base of the neck; the thymus, found in the chest above the heart; the pair of adrenal glands, which are on top of the kidneys; and the gonads, or sex glands.

Nature has equipped us with these endocrine glands to protect us in times of emergency. For example, when we see a tiny youngster or defenseless animal being beaten mercilessly by a sadistic adult, we get angry. This emotion causes our adrenal glands to secrete more adrenaline into our bloodstream, and we get the extra "lift" we need to deal with the situation. The same reaction takes place when we become frightened by threatening people or things, or by various unconscious fears.

Our body is a marvelous machine constructed by nature to meet "natural" situations, and it serves us perfectly only when we put it to proper or "natural" use. When our anger is natural anger, as in the example above, our entire body responds in a natural, temporary way. However, when we lead an unnatural life that causes us continuous stress and strain and puts a perpetual "emergency call" upon our body, we do great harm to ourselves. The constant overstimulation of our endocrine glands drains our life energy. Let us study a few examples and see what this overstimulation does to us.

When we are exposed to heat, cold, high altitudes, starvation, or overexertion, our pituitary gland produces STH, a hormone that wards off the stress of these experiences. However, when we *constantly* experience such stressful emotions and our pituitary gland *overproduces* STH, it causes damaging effects such as fatigue, asthma, diabetes, and other illnesses. STH, it has been discovered, is also overproduced when we have dark, despairing emotions.

When we are constantly aggressively negative, like the boss who is always yelling at subordinates, the unpleasant emotions in the boss can cause an overproduction of another hormone, ACTH, which produces peptic ulcers, a variety of diabetes, and a condition referred to as "protein starvation."

What does all this mean? It means that there is more to illness than meets the eye and that the causes of innumerable illnesses (some doctors claim all) are negative emotions that cause damage to our bodies. Is this to say that we must never experience negative emotions? Certainly not—as long as we live, we will have to face natural emergencies that will affect us emotionally. The point to remember is that we cannot enjoy a life of health, happiness, and success while in a state of constant emotional emergency. We alcoholics cannot live with unrelenting stress and strain. We must face life with pleasant thoughts that produce pleasant emotions. These are as important to us as air, food, and water.

Lesson 5
The Impact of Bad Habits

By now we know that unpleasant emotions cause unhappiness, illness, and even death, and that pleasant emotions produce happiness and ease. If this is true, why do so many people allow themselves to experience unpleasant emotions? Why are they always so tense and strained? Why do they perpetually criticize and complain? Many people are unaware that their unpleasant emotions have disastrous effects upon their health.

Now that we realize that our bad emotions have caused considerable damage to our endocrine glands and nervous systems, we must learn to live the healthful way: by responding to all situations in a pleasant and constructive manner.

Learning to live with pleasant emotions requires conscious effort. In some cases, we might have to completely change our usual reactions and many of our opinions about life. We did not become negative overnight; uncovering and breaking bad thinking habits will take time. Self-study will help us accomplish this. Once we replace our bad thinking patterns with right thinking, we will experience improved health, feelings of ease, and a sense of well-being. In addition, our increasing self-knowledge will bring us greater self-control.

Through self-study, we will learn that all of our emotional troubles began in early childhood and that drinking was just one more bad emotional adjustment to an earlier life full of bad adjustments. This is true even of that scarce alcoholic who became drunk the very first time he had a drink. This individual's bloodstream was so poisoned by hormonal secretions caused by overstimulation from bad emotions that he was a "sitting duck" for alcoholism. In every case, alcoholic patterns begin in childhood. The maladjustment to life and the inability to solve problems eventually evolve into a drinking pattern. The following analogy might help us understand why this is true.

When a man walks a tightrope, he must keep his balance or else he will meet with disaster. All of life is such a tightrope. Lose our balance, and we likewise meet with disaster. Balance is right action that stimulates our body in a manner

17

that brings health and ease. If we are thrown off balance emotionally, we become tense, unhappy, and worried.

This need to achieve balance applies to situations in each person's life; it is the essential quality for right action. Just as the world's nations operate according to their power, so do we individually. We operate on the power of our health and the power of our mind, which influence our actions. Just as populations are constantly growing and changing, so are we as a result of our thinking and actions. We either grow healthier, happier, and more successful, or the opposite occurs. There is only one right way to live: it is to build every day a greater balance of health, happiness, and success for ourselves. This does not mean that we must "keep up with the Joneses." Quite the contrary, it means that we must not let ourselves lose balance. If this happens, we become upset. The emotionally upset state brings unhappiness, an unpleasant emotion that produces illness.

When we were children and did things we weren't supposed to, we had various ways of trying to avoid trouble. At times, we "got away with murder" and temporarily escaped punishment or discernment of our wrong actions, but we did something else too. We built an imbalance for our future. We started bad habit patterns that would throw us off balance in our adult lives. Before we review examples of this, let us consider the importance of balance in other areas of our lives.

Let us say we play tennis or handball. During these games, it is necessary to remain in balance, or to always have control of the center of the court. By always being in the middle, the player has control of both ends. Let us apply this to life. When we have a goal, that goal is a certain distance from where we are at the time. Our job is to jockey ourselves carefully from where we are right now to where we want to go, being careful always to remain in balance on the way.

The same applies to every game of action. As youngsters, most of us arm wrestled at least once. The idea was to throw the other person off balance. So it goes with life. In a social situation, if we are asked a question that throws us off balance, we might become embarrassed. If we fail to have an adequate bank balance, we will face financial disaster. If we become ill and require an operation, we will die if we do not have a balance or reserve of health to fall back upon for recuperation. If we are studying a new subject that requires intense application and concentration, and we don't have both qualities, we will fail to learn.

If we want health, happiness, and success, we must have a balance in those areas of our lives that are concerned with these things. If we want health, we must build a reserve of energy. If we want happiness, we must rid ourselves of the thoughts, emotions, and actions that create unhappiness. If we want success, we must decide how to bring it about and take constructive action to get started. If we are unhappy and do not know why, we are out of balance. We need to study ourselves to find the "why" of our unhappy state and take the corrective action. If we are unhappy and *do* know why, yet still do nothing about it, we are also out of balance. We need courage and perseverance to take the necessary action to correct our situation. Either imbalanced state is equally bad.

The secret of life is balance and action. In order to keep our balance, we must always jockey for better position. Nothing in life stands still, and we must grow stronger with the times. This is the law of evolution. We either evolve or pass into oblivion. There are no two ways about it.

TO LEAD A BALANCED LIFE:

1. BUILD A RESERVE OF ENERGY.

2. THINK POSITIVELY (be optimistic, cheerful, etc.).

3. MAKE LOGICAL PLANS.

4. ACT CONSTRUCTIVELY.

There are alcoholics who begin recovery but fail to attain balance. They exist unhappily with superficial sobriety. Their failure comes from not putting forth the proper effort to live a balanced life. There is no crime in failure, but it seems a crime to stop trying when you have been shown the way.

Those of us who honestly and sincerely discipline ourselves reap a fine harvest from the new patterns we adopt. As in all natural growth, the harvest takes time. Through careful cultivation, we must pull out any unwanted growths. Many of these unwanted bad habits were planted during our childhoods. They resulted from either too lenient or too stern parenting.

Our responses to our parents' actions were ones of imbalance if we purposely deceived our parents, for example, or if we withdrew into a shell or shirked our duties, etc. As we grew, this imbalance became part of us, and with enough of these bad habits, we became extremists. If we successfully lied at home, we became seasoned liars. If bullying worked, we became bullies. If excuses worked, we cultivated the habit of excusing ourselves. If we were babied at home, we grew up to be babies. If we were abused, we grew up to be angry adults. If we were not taken to task for our wrongdoings or failures, we grew up failing to meet our responsibilities. The examples could go on for pages.

Thus the poorly adjusted child can become an alcoholic extremist who drinks to ease the pain of unpleasant situations. When this alcoholic becomes sober through AA, she is still in a state of imbalance until she learns how to make needed emotional adjustments. Real sobriety is the state of balance; superficial sobriety is partial imbalance; alcoholism is disastrous imbalance. Each of us must jockey carefully toward a more balanced position. There is only one way to do this: self-analysis. In self-analysis we discover our *motives* and our *thought patterns.* We must assess where we are now, decide where we want to go, make logical plans to get there, and then go into action. The following lessons will clarify each of these steps, so we can make progress in a logical manner.

Lesson 6
The Need to Investigate Our Past Unpleasant Emotions

We have learned that right thinking is essential for real sobriety. This right thinking brings pleasant emotions. To sustain these pleasant emotions, we've included exercises in these lessons to help eliminate depression and calm our minds. The exercises bring increased energy and optimism. The periodic bouts of depression, and the confusion, lack of energy, aches and pains, and "dry drunks" will gradually disappear. The alcoholic with real sobriety no longer has to contend with these conditions.

We might now ask what makes the difference between superficial and real sobriety. The condition of the mind makes the difference, for the condition of our mind affects our body. The proof is the increased happiness we feel when experiencing good emotions. Each of us can prove this point when we obtain progressively better control of our mind and experience constantly improving health while pursuing self-analysis.

The difference between a drinking alcoholic and an alcoholic with real sobriety is this: the drinking alcoholic has a body that is controlled by a distracted mind, while the serene alcoholic has a mind that has firm control of his body. The alcoholic's compulsion to drink is the result of conditioning. The more he drinks, the greater the compulsion becomes. One drink causes him to have another, and each succeeding drink sets up a "demand" for more by his nervous system. When the mind gives in, the body gains control. This is scientifically true, as will be explained in a forthcoming lesson on alcoholic conditioning.

The superficially sober alcoholic who has been dry in the stomach for years might still be suffering the unfortunate conditions described earlier. What does she have to do to attain the wonderful state of real sobriety? She must purify her body and gain control over her mind. All aches and pains, depressions, and confusion will then disappear. Can alcoholics do this without professional help? If we can understand and apply the lessons in this book, they will lead us toward real sobriety without the need for professional counseling. After all, those of us who are studying these lessons have anywhere from one and a half to fifteen years or more of sobriety. These lessons are designed for people who have been with AA for at least one year, although anyone can benefit from applying them.

There are methods that we can use in our lives to eliminate depression, improve our health, and strengthen our self-control. We will learn about these methods and then apply them in a logical manner. First, in order to gain confidence in their workability, we must understand the scientific principles behind these methods. This conforms to the tradition of not asking anyone to accept anything on the basis of another person saying it is so. We will begin by investigating the reasons for self-analysis.

You may ask, "Why this constant mention of self-analysis? I have been sober for many years and thought I was getting along fine." We suggest that you ask yourself whether you are enjoying ease, calmness, freedom from aches and pains, exceptionally good health, self-control, and happiness, all of which accompany real sobriety. If you are enjoying all of these, our self-analysis studies are not necessary. If you are not, you would be wise to progress toward real sobriety. Until you attain this state, you will never gain all the health and happiness that life has to offer.

We can now proceed with self-analysis and gain an understanding of our past actions. "Why bother to investigate the past?" some might ask. "Why not let the past be the past?" Because, I would answer, everything we have thought, said, and done is still with us. As long as it is with us, it will cause sickness and suffering. Where is this past? It is in our mind. We will prove this by referring to scientific findings. We will show that our past thoughts, words, and deeds stay with us until they are released. We will show that our mind is a kind of tape recorder that records and stores everything that has made an impression upon us.

Dr. Wilder Penfield was a former director of the Montreal Neurological Institute in Montreal, Canada. For more than twenty years, Dr. Penfield performed surgery and research on the human brain. His work proved that humans must have a mind that stores past events, that our so-called mind does indeed exist (although it cannot be seen or touched), and that our memory is part of our brain. How was this discovered?

Dr. Penfield was once operating on a woman's brain when the woman began to talk as if she were giving birth to a child. The woman had been a mother already for many years, and was reliving a past childbirth. What was going on? During the operation, an electrode had been applied to a certain part of the woman's brain, triggering her talk of being in labor. A true scientist, Dr. Penfield was not content to believe that this proved the existence of a mind. He proceeded to touch various parts of the woman's brain, and she began to relive other events.

Still, this was not enough for Dr. Penfield. He spent more than twenty years carrying on such research, eventually proving that different areas of the brain store different past experiences. One area stores sounds. Other areas store certain types of images, and so on. Our brain is compartmentalized, and different types of memories are kept in different places. Both happy and unhappy events remain with us. The more intense our experience, the more vivid our memory of it.

Are Dr. Penfield's findings important to alcoholics? Indeed, they are! They should convince us of our need to carry on self-analysis. Although we have stopped drinking, until we rid ourselves of the unpleasant emotions behind our drinking, these emotions will remain buried in our minds. Since our memory stores events in layers, with the latest event on top, we are not usually aware of our past unhappiness. Nature kindly allows us to forget. Unless we have released them through analysis of some kind, the causes of that unhappiness are probably still within us. The continued presence of past unhappy events explains why so many of us have been ill since we stopped drinking. Those of us who still suffer depression, aches and pains, and unhappy memories are the victims of our minds, which houses our memory patterns. Those memory patterns will continue to plague us until they are removed.

There are two kinds of control we can take over our memories: First, we can create a pleasant future memory by controlling our present thinking. Second, we must find a way to release the unpleasant events stored in our memory; these memories will remain until we learn how to release them.

To create a future pleasant memory, we must always be conscious of the harmful effects of unpleasant thoughts, which cause unpleasant emotions, as previously explained. We must also learn the technique of pleasant thinking and to live life pleasantly. Then, to acquire control of our memory, we must know a little about what our mind is, what it does, and why it is important to us. Our knowledge of these things must be based in physiology, psychology, anatomy, and medicine.

We must carry on self-analysis because we must *understand* our past actions in order to control our present and future behavior and improve our health. We must *learn to live with pleasant emotions* that bring health, happiness, and success. We must *acquire the knowledge of how to live a balanced way of life* in order to do this. However, while we are learning this, we must also *release the unhappy past from our minds* in order to be free of the tensions and poisons created by the unpleasant emotions of this unhappy past. Until released, the past will continue to resurface, and we will suffer emotionally induced illnesses until we die.

WHY DO SELF-ANALYSIS?

—TO UNDERSTAND OUR PAST ACTIONS

—TO CONTROL OUR PRESENT ACTIONS

—TO DIRECT OUR FUTURE BEHAVIOR

—TO IMPROVE OUR HEALTH

Lesson 7
The Importance of
Understanding Our Fears

We learned in lesson 6 that we must do two things if we are to be happy. First, we must learn the science of living in a pleasant manner. Second, we must learn how to release the tensions of the unhappy past. Both require that we change ourselves.

There's an old saying that you can't teach an old dog new tricks. It's true only if you believe it, for old dogs actually have been taught new tricks. The best example of this happened during World War II, when dogs were trained to be vicious for combat. After the war was over, the dogs were unconditioned and returned to their owners, docile and obedient.

An "old dog" can be taught new tricks, providing the conditioning is strong enough. All learning is a matter of conditioning that creates either good or bad habits. Habits develop from how a person begins life and progresses through life. If a person cultivates enough bad habits to throw himself off balance, then he must eventually recondition himself by replacing bad habits with good habits. This is simple but not easy, but it must be done to acquire health and happiness.

One of the worst bad habits we alcoholics have is allowing ourselves to live with fear. We can develop the habit of living with fear merely by continuously having fearful thoughts. Fear can be cultivated, and it is this cultivation that harms people every day. These people are conditioning themselves with innumerable unpleasant emotions. This is characteristic of every alcoholic.

There are all kinds of fear, and we alcoholics seem to have experienced most kinds. Some of us had a fear of physical harm. Some of us were afraid of criticism, and some were afraid we would fail in our undertakings. Some had hidden fears and anxieties. Although the alcoholic fear patterns vary, they all have one thing in common: they are examples of negative emotions.

Why did we suffer these fears? The answer is that we found ourselves in a situation for which we had no solution, no way out. Not being able to face our problems and escape the unpleasant situation, we became fearful, then drank to ease our pain.

When we entered AA and committed ourselves to the program, many of the fears related to our drinking disappeared, at least temporarily. Those of us who believe in a Higher Power gave up our fears to that Higher Power. It is said that fear is present when God is absent. So we can conclude that the opposite of fear is faith. The alcoholic is unsure of herself in many ways because she lacks faith in herself or in someone or something. She drinks to escape the pain of facing the unpleasantness that results from this situation. When she enters AA and begins to return to a balanced life, she must still face the problem of retracing her steps to find out when fear first entered her life and where her conditioning went wrong.

When the sober alcoholic analyzes his fears, he realizes that fear is about the unknown. The more he learns about himself and life, the less he has to fear. Fear is greater where ignorance is greater, and fear is less where knowledge is greater. The knowledge an alcoholic needs is self-knowledge, because alcoholic fears arise from a lack of self-understanding. Our personal inadequacies caused us to suffer various unpleasant emotions. These emotions caused ever-increasing tensions that we tried to ease with alcohol. Instead of anesthetizing our pain, we anesthetized our minds. As we drank, our fears seemed to disappear, when actually they were growing. They did not diminish until we stopped drinking and began to change our alcoholic thinking.

Alcoholic fears are not always obvious, but each of us has a certain number of them. We condition ourselves to be fearful. It is one thing to be cautious and careful; it is another thing to live in constant fear of dire events or circumstances that are not likely to ever become reality. One is reasonable. The other is irrational, unpleasant, harmful thinking.

Much research has been conducted on the relationship between fear and alcoholism. Psychologists Masserman and Yum of Yale University believed that fear (or a conflict induced by fear) could motivate a person to choose an alcoholic solution instead of avoiding it. Experimenting on cats rather than human beings, they showed that fear is involved in producing a preference for alcohol. The preference is reinforced in one or more ways. First, the alcohol reduces the strength of fear. Second, it reduces the strength of the stimulation that produced the fear, or the conflict produced by the fear.

If psychological experiments show that when cats are afraid, they are more prone to escaping into alcohol than facing the fear without it, does the same apply to human beings? Let's take a look at two typical examples, each showing how people use alcohol to cope with fear.

First, suppose a man has to tell his family the unhappy news that he lost his job. The alcoholic will take a drink before speaking in order to reduce the intensity of his fear of his family's reaction. Then there's the woman who has been severely reprimanded by her boss. In her apartment later that evening, she takes a drink to soften the memory of the earlier upsetting scene with her employer. She hopes a drink will help her to "handle" her fears.

Whether or not we agree with the results of the experiments by Masserman and Yum, we must all agree that it is not enough that we simply stay away from that first drink. We must not allow ourselves to become fearful enough to want to escape into that drink in the first place. Learning the technique of conquering fear is part of these lessons.

All unpleasant emotions have some basis in fear, whether it is obvious or subtle. Unless a person believes herself to be completely fearless, she must have fears of some kind. Whenever the situation she is afraid of arises, she is prone to suffering these fears. Whenever she does not place faith in a Higher Power or ultimate authority of some kind, she is susceptible to fears associated with problems she cannot solve and situations she cannot deal with. Acknowledging that we have certain fears is the first step to overcoming them. Then, the next wise and healthy step is doing the analysis necessary to eliminate our fears.

An excellent study that shows the relationship between emotionally induced illness and fear took place in 1949 at Cornell University. A sheep, part of a flock standing in a field, was put through a series of electric shocks intended to induce fear and apprehension. A wire was tied around one leg of the sheep, and for one week it walked around experiencing no electric shocks. The second week, electricity was run through the wire. The sheep's leg twitched visibly with each shock, but the sheep was relatively undisturbed and went on eating.

The third week, a bell was rung ten seconds before each shock. The resulting fear and apprehension caused severe illness in the sheep. The shock was made stronger and monotonously repetitive. When the sheep now heard the bell, it stopped eating and waited apprehensively for the shock. This repetition of the bell ringing, followed by the shock, continued until finally (1) the sheep stopped eating, (2) it followed the other sheep around the field, (3) it quit walking, (4) it could not stand on its feet, and (5) it breathed with difficulty. The repetition of the unpleasant emotions of fear, anxiety, and apprehension brought this sheep to the verge of breakdown. Had these monotonous, unpleasant emotions continued, the sheep would have died. As soon as the shocks were discontinued, the sheep returned to normal (Schindler 1954).

This experiment shows how the mind, animal or human, can be conditioned. The outcome of the conditioning depends upon the emotions used for the conditioning. If the conditioning is done with pleasant emotions, the results are health and happiness. If the emotions are unpleasant, the results are disease and unhappiness.

Each of us must consider our personal histories and ask ourselves, "Am I conditioning myself with unpleasant emotions? What makes me fearful? What am I afraid of? Why do I feel tense and strained?" These and similar questions are a necessary part of self-analysis.

Analysis is necessary to every successful enterprise. In politics, we "look at the record," or study the history of the individual or company, etc. In scientific research, we experiment, test, and analyze. In business, we examine the profit and loss sheet. So it should be with our personal life. We should examine our past and our present and benefit by our mistakes. Until we do this, our past will be repressed, always ready to disturb us when we are least able to cope with it. Until we really know why we drank, we will lack the understanding we need to prevent an inadvertent slip. This understanding and freedom from fear come only from self-analysis. We can never understand ourselves by postponing self-examination. We must look at ourselves objectively, accept what we see, and start from there to build the life we desire. This is the way to health and happiness.

Lesson 8
The Three Steps to Real Sobriety

So far we have learned that alcoholism is a psychosomatic illness that begins with negative thoughts of fear, based on anxiety. These negative thoughts cause negative emotions through the operation of our autonomic nervous system, which automatically delivers every thought and emotion-message to the nerve, organ, or gland concerned with that thought and emotion. We cannot control this automatic action. To improve our mental and physical health, we must control our thinking. We must prevent the flow of negative thoughts that cause mental and physical disintegration.

When we give in to negative thoughts that automatically cause unpleasant emotions, various nerves, glands, and organs in our bodies become overstimulated, resulting in tension and oversecretion of hormones. When a person continuously thinks the same negative thoughts, she sets up a vicious cause-and-effect chain reaction of negative emotions that wears her down, day after day. Eventually, she falls victim to one or more psychosomatic illnesses. Alcoholism may be one of them.

People respond to negative emotions in different ways. The alcoholic drinks. The following is the way it happens. First, the alcoholic suffers unpleasant emotions of fear, based on worry or anxiety. He has a choice to fight or run away. He mentally runs away, easing his tension by drinking. At first this escape works fine, and he gets into the habit of drinking to ease the tension caused by unpleasant emotions. Of course, the drinking does not solve his problems; it merely anesthetizes his mind. His problems remain, and he keeps drinking to ease his tension and pain. The more he drinks, the greater his compulsion to drink becomes. This is due to the action of his autonomic nervous system.

This chain of events happens because the alcoholic has a peculiar kind of temperament that makes it difficult for him to face his problems or himself. As he drinks, his problems continue to mount. He is not able to resolve his original problems, and the drinking creates additional problems. Soon problem solving becomes impossible. His relationships with family, friends, and working associ-

29

ates deteriorate. He drinks more and more compulsively because of these strained relationships. He goes downhill rapidly in every way, which causes him more worry. More worry creates more tension. More tension increases his compulsion to drink. By this time, he is drinking automatically to ease his pain.

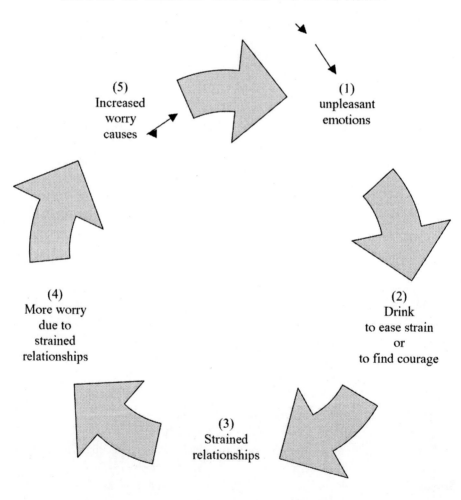

THE DRINKING CYCLE

(5)
Increased
worry
causes

(1)
unpleasant
emotions

(4)
More worry
due to
strained
relationships

(2)
Drink
to ease strain
or
to find courage

(3)
Strained
relationships

The causes of alcoholism are most complex when a person's inability to face life in a normal way goes back to early childhood. A person who becomes alcoholic in later life (he might not take his first drink until late adulthood), might not have the faintest idea what is behind his drinking. He will never know until he first gets dry in the stomach. After this, he must get clear in the head.

What does all this mean? It means that no alcoholic is normal just because he is no longer drinking. Becoming completely cured of this disease requires knowing why we drank in the first place. How can we become mentally and physically healthy until we can face life in a balanced manner? The classic phrase "know thyself" applies to no one more than the alcoholic. To stop drinking is not enough. We must go all the way back, find out what went wrong, pick up the lost pieces of our personality, put them together, and start in a new and proper direction. Failure to do this results in failure to obtain complete recovery, or the state of real sobriety.

Alcoholics fall into five categories:
(1) Those who drink themselves to death;
(2) Those who become institutionalized due to the damage done to mind and body;
(3) Those, institutionalized or not, who eventually get dry with the help of AA;
(4) Those who stop their drinking through some means other than AA; and
(5) Those who, upon becoming dry in the stomach, decide that they must also get clear in the head. They can do this through psychiatry, psychology, psychoanalysis, psychotherapy, or individual self-analysis.

The last method, individual self-analysis, is what these lessons are all about. We believe there is no reason that any nondrinking alcoholic who is able to read and apply these lessons cannot analyze himself and remove the need for professional counseling.

AA is one of the greatest movements of modern times. Carrying on the tradition of AA, these lessons teach the psychology of sobriety and the science of applying the Twelve Steps. We believe that no alcoholic can really get sober and become well-adjusted unless she lives a spiritual life based upon reason. The word *spirituality* here should not be construed as applying to any particular religion. It is used as the word meaning the opposite of materialism, or seeking only material gain. The alcoholic suffered the stress and strain of a maladjusted life that was contrary to her true nature. She must find her true nature before she can be truly happy and well-adjusted, both materially and spiritually. Our approach to mental and physical health must come from looking "within," which is the spiritual approach.

The Twelve Steps contain the wisdom we need in our pursuit of mental and physical health. These lessons teach the science of applying the steps successfully to our lives.

For example, in AA we are told to take daily inventory. Who among us cannot use more help with our inventory? Knowing what is wrong with our thinking must come first if we are to change wrong living to right living. What is another word for inventory? That word is self-analysis. We analyze our failures, weaknesses, and shortcomings. Then we make ourselves physically and mentally well by the application of scientific methods especially developed for alcoholics by alcoholics.

By doing our daily self-inventory and practicing daily relaxation (presented in lesson 10), we will be on our way to greater conscious self-control. We would be wise to incorporate another aspect of our own Twelve Steps: daily meditation (the Eleventh Step). To do this, we relax the body (explained in lesson 10) and turn our mind to the Higher Power. Then, by combining all these practices with our positive thinking, we are on the road to health and happiness.

Obtaining real sobriety requires understanding the psychology of sobriety. It also means having some knowledge of physics, physiology, anatomy, and psychosomatic medicine. This course condenses this knowledge into logical, easy-to-understand lessons that guide alcoholics through the three steps to real sobriety. In the first step, we find the causes of our unhappiness, pain, and problems by taking a complete inventory of our negative emotions. Next, we apply the scientific methods learned in these lessons to rebuild our mental and physical health. Finally, we use our newfound energy to obtain our desires and goals.

Three Steps to Real Sobriety

Step 1

Do self-analysis to discover negative emotions that rob our energy, damage our health, disturb our mind.

Step 2

Rebuild mental and physical energy by applying principles learned in these lessons.

Step 3

Use newfound health and peaceful mind to attain our goals.

Lesson 9
Three Formulas

Not all alcoholics are sincerely interested in learning about the relationship between the mind and alcoholism. We who are studying these lessons want to know the truth about ourselves and are willing to do the hard work of self-analysis to obtain self-understanding.

The average alcoholic talks a lot and resigns himself to a "do-little life" by justifying his actions with the statement that at least he is sober. But we go a step further. We choose not to live with fear, for fear leads us to drinking. We refuse to live in fear of taking that first drink. We intend to get rid of our fears, not merely repress them more deeply into our minds.

Those who apply these lessons want to improve themselves; others, deep down, are afraid to try.

There are three formulas, or thought processes, which will help us on the path to true sobriety.

The first formula, below, must become an integral part of our daily thinking:

To make a thing possible, we must first desire it.

The first step in overcoming problems is positive thinking. What happens to us depends on what is going on in our minds. Positive thinking produces positive actions, and positive actions can bring positive results. Negative thinking gets negative results. We must train ourselves to think positively.

For example, when we find ourselves caught in a traffic jam or a long checkout line, our reaction should no longer be one of growling frustration. Instead we should use the sudden extra time to relax, greet others cheerfully, and accept peacefully the things we cannot control. After all, if we want to overcome our problems, will not calmness and optimism get us farther than anger and negativity? In every daily situation, we must *desire* to think in a positive way.

Now let us consider the second formula for daily living:

What we desire, we must believe exists for us now.

We must believe that positive thinking exists for us now, that we *can do it.* These formulas are scientifically true. But proving them requires the student to be open-minded. Remember that "as you think, so shall it be." As the existence of psychosomatic illnesses shows, a person can become ill from his own negative thinking.

See if you can find an alcoholic who got that way without thinking negatively. Where there is alcoholism, there is always negativism, which breeds unhappiness, ill health, and lack of success. There cannot be real sobriety without complete positive thinking. This is why our first job is to discontinue negative thinking. We must believe in ourselves and act upon our belief: we *do* practice positive thinking *constantly.*

Now we are at the third formula for daily thinking:

The mind is like a magnet. It attracts what it is concentrating on.

This statement recalls the saying "like attracts like." But do we fully understand the truth of this statement? Suppose a magnet is placed on the floor and tacks are scattered nearby. As the magnet faces the tacks, the tacks are attracted to the magnet. In the same way, suppose John spots Mary across the room and is enchanted by her. He can't help staring. She senses this and turns toward him. John's mind turned in Mary's direction, and her mind responded. It's the same for us. If we envision health and happiness, our minds turn in that direction. We draw positive results. So if we know that negative thinking causes unhappiness and illness, why do we continue such thinking? It is from habit.

We must now make a conscious effort to control our daily thinking. To do so, we must know the direction our thinking is taking. If it is negative, we must change direction. Because of our old bad thinking habits, this will not be easy. But as we continue trying to change our thinking pattern day after day, it will become easier, and we will find ourselves becoming more and more relaxed. Why? Doing the right thing at the right time becomes more and more automatic through the practice of conscious thought control.

First we develop the habit of positive thinking. Right thinking produces right action. Then, through right action, we gain self-confidence and become more relaxed.

Assignment 1

Purchase a diary immediately. You will use it to conduct an honest daily self-analysis.

You will record observations about yourself honestly and objectively.

For the next seven days, do the following without fail. Each morning upon getting up, put on your robe and sit in some quiet place. Calm your mind, and plan your day.

Next, determine then and there that you are going to think and act in a pleasant manner all day long, no matter what happens. Having done this, repeat this statement **ten times:**

I believe that everything will go well for me today. I turn my life over to the Higher Power. I know God helps those who help themselves, and I will do my part to make this come true. Today I make every thought a pleasant thought and every act a pleasant act.

Each evening in the quiet of your own mind, think about the improvements you have made in controlling your negative thinking. Examine your day.

1. Review the morning. Examine your actions, your reactions. Was there any negative thinking?

2. Review the afternoon. Examine your actions, your reactions. Was there any negative thinking?

3. Record your reactions honestly in your diary. Give yourself a percentage mark for the day. Do you deserve 100 percent, 90 percent, 80 percent?

1st day: Percentage_____   5th day: Percentage_____

2nd day: Percentage_____   6th day: Percentage_____

3rd day: Percentage_____   7th day: Percentage_____

4th day: Percentage_____   *Remember: God helps those who help themselves.*

Lesson 10
Understanding the I

The drinking alcoholic cannot cope with the difficulties of everyday life. In the past, through the wrong use of his mind, he caused his body to suffer. Now, in order to improve his health and mind control, he must follow a logical plan to create the life he desires.

Before continuing, it is important we understand what is meant by the *conscious mind.* The scriptures of all religions discuss the conscious mind, but they refer to it as the *soul* or *spirit.* We shall refer to it as the *I* in each of us. No person in the universe is the same as another. Each of us is a unique atom of personality among the endless variety of atoms of personality that comprises humankind.

Just as we are *I* to ourselves, everybody around us is *I* to himself or herself. Thus *I* can refer only to the self. When someone else says *I,* he is talking only about himself. *I* is entirely personal and individual. It belongs to us alone and sets us apart from everyone else. No one else can see this *I* or feel its emotions or express its desires. It is our personal, individual spirit or nature that is the real us. This is the *I* we must come to understand if we are to enjoy real happiness and excellent health.

To know the *I* is the first step in developing the mind. People who are disturbed or distracted or unhappy, feel this way because the *I* in them is unhappy. They are discontented because they are acting against their real nature. Deep down something may be gnawing away at them, but because of mental blocks, they may be unable to look deep within to find out the trouble. Psychiatrists, psychoanalysts, and psychologists help clients who can no longer think in a logical manner. When people turn to outside help, the *I* of their counselors becomes their identity and thinking process. The counselor's *I* (his or her consciousness or spirit) looks into the subconscious mind of the client, which holds the clue to understanding the disturbance. In time, we will do this for ourselves to attain self-understanding. But first we must know better this thing called *I* and how we can use it psychologically to our advantage.

Let us clarify what we have read so far by asking:

In my job, what am I?

In my family life, what am I?

In my spare time, what am I?

For the sake of illustration, let us give these answers:

In my job, I am a fireman.

In my family life, I am a husband and father.

In my spare time, I am an amateur photographer.

To answer these questions, the *I* must say "I am." In the answers, the *I* identifies with being a fireman, a husband, a father, and an amateur photographer. Thus, when we desire something (such as to be a fireman, husband, etc.), we must identify the *I* in us with the particular thing we want. In the same way, when we are unhappy, it is because the *I* in us selected conditions that make us unhappy. If our actions are wrong, or if our situation is opposed to our real nature, we can never be happy. We have all heard stories of a dominating parent forcing a child into an occupation against the child's true nature. There is the familiar example of the son forced to take over the family business instead of being allowed to fulfill his heart's desire to become a doctor. This young man, like all of us, can find happiness when he is able to satisfy his real nature, his real *I*.

Try as we might, we cannot think about ourselves without referring to the *I* in us, although the majority of people go about trying to fool their *I*. The average man or woman does not know himself or herself, and thus he or she is not really happy, and may be most unhappy. Ignorance of self makes misery and misfits.

Does this apply to each of us? Yes. We wouldn't have become alcoholics if we had not started to drink. If we had been thinking rationally, we would have sat down and examined the *I* and asked ourselves: "Why do I need this alcohol? Why am I unhappy? Why am I tense? Why do I need stimulants to ease me? Why am I not satisfied with myself?" Providing we were rational and could get deep enough to understand ourselves, the right answers to these questions would have come from the *I*.

No one but the *I* has the right answer. The trouble with the unhappy, distressed, confused person—and the alcoholic is no exception—is that he cannot get *to* himself. And, until he can, he can never express his real self—the *I*. Until he can, he will suffer tensions, constrictions, fears, anxieties, worries, and so on because he will be serving things other than the real *I*, and these things will cause unhappiness. In plain English, he will continue to fight himself and feel anguish.

Is there any substitution for the painful process of getting to know the *I* in us? No. The *I* must be found and fulfilled. And until it is, we can never be truly happy. Until we uncover our real nature, we will continue to reach out for everything that is new and different in the hope of finding something satisfying and fulfilling. This is living life the hard way. As the scriptures tell us, "Be still" (Psalm 46:10). Psychologically, the only way for us to find health and happiness is to investigate our honest desires and free ourselves from false desires demanded by our senses. These false desires are a result of our bad habits.

Our compulsion to drink at one time seemed a logical demand to us, for we felt that we could not get along without alcohol. Later on, we found that this compulsion coexisted with other bad habits. If we could have gone deep within ourselves then, we would have learned the real reason for our drinking—that we wanted to escape something distasteful. With most alcoholics, that distasteful thing is the very thing that each of us must do: look into ourselves and see and accept who we really are, our true self, and proceed to be that which we were inherently made to be.

Does this mean that if we are unhappy in our jobs, we quit? Of course not. Neither does it suggest quitting any other activity we are involved in. Instead, we must right the wrongs we have done to our nature, in a logical way, taking the AA route of "first things first." We must please our true natures, but we must change our lives in a logical way. We are no longer slaves to emotions. Instead, we are followers of logic. We are going to better ourselves in every way, mentally, physically, and materially. But we must follow the logical path that each of us is going to set up after we use honest self-study to acquire a better understanding of our personal requirements. This is the only way we are ever going to enjoy that thing called happiness. And this is the only way that we are ever going to enjoy health, for health and happiness go together.

Assignment 2

Assignment 1 is to be done each morning and evening for a week.

Assignment 2 is to be accomplished each morning, from now on, before assignment 1. The new assignment can also serve as a relaxation exercise at any time of day. It will relax every nerve and calm the mind.

There is a definite relationship between respiration and calmness of mind. The mind calms in direct proportion to the slowness and deepness of respiration. Slowing the respiration and the movement of the mind increases the ability to concentrate.

Sit upright in a chair, your eyes closed, and rest your arms and hands on your thighs.

1. Try to make your mind a complete blank.

2. With all of your power, concentrate on your feet. Make them relax by mentally relaxing them. Tell yourself, "I *relax* my feet. My feet are completely relaxed."

3. When you feel that your feet are relaxed, move up to your calves. Make them relax, as you did in step 2.

4. Using the same method, relax your thighs.

5. Concentrate on your trunk. Relax your chest, abdomen, and back, in that order.

6. Concentrate on your hands and arms and relax them.

7. Finally, relax your head and neck. Keep your eyes closed.

Now that you are completely relaxed, you are ready for the next phase of this exercise. Your eyes will remain closed for this entire exercise. Concentrate all of your mental power on the center of your forehead, right between your eyes. While doing this, be certain that all of your energy has been pulled from every other part of your body and that you are concentrating all of this power at the center of your forehead.

Now, inhale slowly and deeply and evenly, counting slowly 1, 2, 3, 4.

Hold your breath for the same even count of 1, 2, 3, 4.

Exhale slowly and evenly for the same count of 1, 2, 3, 4.

After you have mastered this part of the exercise, substitute the counting with the following thoughts.

As you inhale, think, "I'm taking in energy."

As you hold your breath, think, "I'm full of energy."

As you exhale, think, "I'm releasing all tension."

Think only of these statements, and nothing else, during this exercise.

Visualize what you are thinking about. *Visualize* taking in energy, being full of energy, and releasing all tension. Some people may visualize the energy as light flowing into their body and enveloping their body, and the tension as black clouds flowing out of their body. People have different ways of visualizing. Find what works for you.

Develop the habit of performing this deep breathing exercise for at least ten minutes at a time. You can use it to ease tension at any time of the day.

Lesson 11
The Importance of Not Dwelling on the Past

We have learned that good thoughts, related to such concepts as agreeableness, courage, and affections, cause pleasant emotions. These pleasant emotions manifest themselves in our bodies through the autonomic nervous system and/or endocrine glands as "optimal stimulation," or that "just right" feeling of health and well-being.

Unpleasant thoughts, related to such concepts as anger, anxiety, and dissatisfaction, cause unpleasant emotions that stimulate the autonomic nervous system and/or endocrine glands and cause chemical and physical changes. These changes are imbalances that manifest themselves as disease. While this resulting disease is emotionally induced, it is nevertheless a definite physical illness, and not imaginary. Emotionally induced illnesses take innumerably different forms, anything from gas pains to asthma, depending on the type and intensity of emotions.

Since different thoughts produce different emotions, each individual might be considered to produce different emotions. And each individual might be considered to be of a different physical and chemical makeup due to his individual life of thought and emotions. Thus no two individuals are exact duplicates in mental and physical makeup. Now we can understand the how and why of individuality and why people differ from one another.

We alcoholics drank as the result of negative emotions caused by negative thinking. Drinking was the effect; thinking was the cause. To be completely sober, the alcoholic must not only stop drinking, he must also stop the cause of drinking—negative thinking. Until he does, he will be subject to dry drunks, depressions, hallucinations, fantasies, failures, and so on. Until he does, he will continue to live in fear of that dreaded first drink. No one can afford to live in fear. Fear is an unpleasant emotion, and constant unpleasant emotions cause emotionally induced illness.

If we should not fear that first drink, then what is the answer? The answer is to live happily without any need for alcohol, for when the compulsion finally disappears—and it will—our past negative life will also disappear, through the release of past emotions.

We cannot afford to live in the past, and too many alcoholics do. Telling our stories is a constructive therapy when we do it to help others. But it is another thing to *dwell* upon dubious past glories, excitements, successes, or failures. Until we release the past, we are shackled by it. The past was not good for us, and to relive the past means to relive either conscious or subconscious unpleasantness. Please note the word *subconscious*, for all memory is subconscious. We may not be conscious of the detrimental effects of dwelling upon the past, but they are there. It is good to recall the past in AA talks and for personal constructive, analytical reasons, but it is unhealthy to dwell continuously on the past just to reminisce.

For a certain length of time, every alcoholic needs the chance to catch her breath, get sober, coast along easily, and get physically well. Finally, the time comes when the alcoholic must stand tall and reach for his or her goal. This is the case in all successful therapies. This "standing tall" means asserting one's individuality, one's *I*, in a practical, optimistic, down-to-earth, consistent, mature, and honest life plan. When this time arrives, the past is past. There is no fear, only fearlessness—not recklessness, but lack of fear. The individual succeeds because she now knows herself thoroughly. She knows her abilities, her capacity, her limitations, and her weaknesses. She is realistic; she is practical; she has fortitude; she does not kid herself. She knows what she wants to do and does it because she enjoys doing it. She is a thoroughly honest, simple, sincere, happy person because she has "found" herself.

To find yourself means losing your past and living your now, according to who you really are now, not who you incorrectly imagined yourself to be in the past. A "rebirth" must take place, and a new life must be lived. A new person—the real individual—must emerge through honest, sincere, fearless self-appraisal and self-analysis. This requires the painful self-crucifixion of our past life, and our resurrection as the new and whole individual through the purification process of self-analysis.

This is simple but not easy. We have all heard that phrase before, and we know what it means. We can apply that phrase to this next step up the ladder on our way to self-knowledge. The first step was to conquer our drinking. This next step is to control our thinking. To do this, we must give up the unpleasant, pain-producing past and live in the "now."

Again, this is simple but not easy. When a person takes away something, he must substitute something in its place. The reason most people dwell upon the past is that the past is all they have. They are afraid to start over, and so all they do is live with their memories. This amounts to fantasy. Unfortunately, too many alcoholics, though sober, go on living in fantasy and never come back to normal life.

For that individual whose past was glorious as well as unhappy, it is difficult to begin again in the now. But this is the path the recovering alcoholic must take in order to build a new life, for there is only now.

And we must begin now, for one minute from now, now will be gone forever.

Assignment 3

The time has come to begin checking yourself and your thinking. Take the daily inventory for two weeks (Assignment 1). Then take the following brief psychological test to compare your attitude with the accepted normal attitudes and behavior patterns.

Bear in mind that *normal* is a debatable concept. However, as far as psychology is concerned, we can admit without objection that there are certain "norms" in behavior patterns.

Answers to the test questions are given at the end of this lesson. These answers correspond to what is considered "normal." This standard psychological test is intended to show you how well you really understand yourself. It is meant for no other purpose. Do not look at the answers until you have finished the test. It is tempting to look ahead, but doing so only defeats the purpose of taking the test. Save your completed test for future reference. Soon you will find yourself reviewing your answers and asking yourself: "Am I the same person who gave these answers?" This experience will happen to you, for this is what self-analysis does for us. It makes us better persons.

This is your first self-analysis test. There will be others. Remember that you are not competing for a good mark but are trying to understand yourself better. No one need ever see your test results or your personal score. So be honest with yourself and answer based on who you actually are, not on who you would like others to see. Read the test instructions closely. Then read each question carefully, thinking each over and asking yourself, "Does this apply to me or doesn't it?" If the statement does apply to you 100 percent, the answer is yes. If not, the answer is no. If you are uncertain, check the "uncertain" column. Uncertainty means that you lack self-knowledge in that particular area.

Self-Knowledge Test 1

Directions: Answer each question by checking the space that represents most accurately your opinion of yourself. For example, if a statement describes you accurately, place a check in the space after *Y.*

Yes No Uncertain

1. I always appreciate frank criticism of my faults   1. Y__ N__ U__

2. I never lack courage when I need it   2. Y__ N__ U__

3. I sometimes criticize others for saying the same thing I myself might say   3. Y__ N__ U__

4. There are times when I am not as clean and well-groomed as I could be   4. Y__ N__ U__

5. Everyone thinks I am an unselfish person   5. Y__ N__ U__

6. I sometimes excuse others for displaying characteristics that are a part of my own personality   6. Y__ N__ U__

7. On occasion I resent new ideas because they do not satisfy me emotionally   7. Y__ N__ U__

8. I have sometimes corrected others when they have irritated me   8. Y__ N__ U__

9. I am grateful for everything given to me   9. Y__ N__ U__

10. I am always courteous to others   10.Y__ N__ U__

11. I sometimes do a good deed with the praise or advantage it will bring me in mind   11.Y__ N__ U__

12. I have never insulted anybody   12.Y__ N__ U__

13. I have never evaded the truth   13.Y__ N__ U__

14. I always describe correctly what I read or see   14.Y__ N__ U__

15. I laugh as readily at myself as I do at other people   15.Y__ N__ U__

16. My personal habits probably annoy some people   16.Y__ N__ U__

17. Occasionally, I think certain thoughts about sex that I would prefer not to reveal to others   17.Y__ N__ U__

Mark yourself as follows:
Give yourself two points for each statement you answered as follows:
Yes: 3, 4, 6, 7, 8, 11, 16, 17

No: 1, 2, 5, 9, 10, 12, 13, 14, 15
For any answer not matching the key above, subtract two points.
For any statement marked "uncertain," there is no score.

Your Self-Knowledge Mark
A score of 20 or more indicates that you have a better-than-average understanding of yourself in most situations.
A score of 14 to 19 indicates that you have an average understanding of yourself.
A score of 9 to 13 indicates that you have a fair understanding of yourself in some situations.
A score below 9 indicates that you lack self-understanding in most instances.
Don't worry if your score is not what you hoped for. This score is your personal baseline from which to progress and improve.

Lesson 12
Peace of Mind

By now we should have a better understanding of ourselves than when these lessons began. When we are genuinely committed to following a clear-cut self-improvement plan, the days fly by. This is a good sign. It shows that we are fully occupied and points to the value of using time wisely. The purpose of these lessons is to rid ourselves of stress and strain. This freedom will come gradually but steadily; it will be the basic ingredient of the new life we are leading. But we should remember that progress will not come unless we practice the twice-daily breathing exercises and concentration exercises.

Before proceeding with a study of *thought*—what it is, and how we can control it—we must discuss peace of mind. Peace of mind is what everybody wants, but just what is it? Peace of mind requires an absence of stress and strain. If we keep ourselves relaxed, we can have peace of mind. Such relaxation requires balance. Balance means that we do not push too hard, that we do not allow ourselves to be under emotional or physical strain.

We do not have this balance now, but it will come step by step. Each time we release hate, resentment, frustration, and fear, we release the accompanying tension. Once we have released sufficient tension, we will earn that coveted peace of mind. Meanwhile, we are releasing old tensions through our breathing exercises, which must accompany our daily autosuggestion exercises (the three formulas) for keeping our emotions pleasant.

While breaking down tensions of the past, we must also learn the technique of knowing ourselves. We have begun to learn it, and we should already be using it to release our tensions, providing we have been taking daily inventory of our unpleasant thoughts, words, and deeds. This is necessary, for unless we are objective and observant when it comes to our thoughts and behavior, we cannot bring about improvement. First, we must know the trouble. Then we must know how to address it. As we make our self-discoveries, we will take the necessary self-improvement steps.

As we proceed, we will develop the technique of analyzing the various areas of our life. The technique is a form of logical analysis. Before we can learn it, however, we must examine the mind, how it works, and how it applies to our personal life. This course both explains the facts of how the mind works and applies these facts to a science of self-therapy.

Self-improvement is a continuously evolving process. Our improvement can only happen as fast as we learn and then apply what we learn. This is a program of action, and we must take the action. This is something no one else can do for us.

Real serenity means having peace of mind, and it includes physical and emotional health. We have already learned that physical health and emotional health are related. Those of us who are unwell got that way because of the lives we have led.

What we are learning is scientifically true: health of mind and body go together. If we know ourselves, we do not fight ourselves. When we stop fighting ourselves, we stop having the conflicting emotions that create inner tensions that rob us of energy. The unpleasant emotions wear down our tissues, overstimulate our glands, and constrict our organs. We learn the right way to live in order to reduce tension and build a storehouse of energy. It is as simple as that, although the scientific explanation will take time to understand. This is why we are proceeding slowly. The mind can accept a limited number of new ideas at a time. Each person should give about 15 minutes to the daily inventory and a half hour each day to apply the breathing exercises and the concentration exercises and discover the benefits. The next four lessons concern a person's conscious thinking, for we must ease the tensions of our everyday life in order to prevent the development of further tensions. In other words, if we can better adjust to situations, the happier and healthier we will be. Practically speaking, all our problems are related to three challenges:

1.   We must be happy about ourselves.

2.   We must feel right about other people.

3.   We must be able to meet the demands of life.

In this lesson, let us consider our personal behavior in relation to our emotional reaction to situations. Let us see what makes us happy or unhappy with ourselves. Remember that (1) we must know our trouble, (2) we must learn how to rectify it, and (3) we must proceed to rectify it.

These lessons help us bring our troubles to light and learn ways to solve them, while we simultaneously release our tensions and build self-confidence, renewed energy, and enthusiasm for life.

Self-Knowledge Test 2

1. A person who feels comfortable about himself does not become overwhelmed by his own emotions. Ask yourself the following questions, checking *yes* or *no*. Save the answers for reference later on.

    Do I "blow my top" often? *YES*___ *NO*___

    Am I angry at someone right now? *YES*___ *NO*___

    Do I fall constantly in and out of love? *YES*___ *NO*___

    Am I jealous of others all the time? *YES*___ *NO*___

    Am I worried about something or someone? *YES*___ *NO*___

    Do I have a feeling of guilt that is bothering me? *YES*___ *NO*___

    Am I afraid of something or someone? *YES*___ *NO*___

    Do I fail to practice "easy does it?" *YES*___ *NO*___

2. When a person is comfortable about herself, she can take life's disappointments in stride. Now ask yourself:

    Do I fail to "roll with the punches" of life? *YES*___ *NO*___

    Do I let little details tie me up in knots? *YES*___ *NO*___

    Do I place too much emphasis on people's promises? *YES*___ *NO*___

    Do I worry too much about what other people think of me? *YES*___ *NO*___

    Do I live too much in the future? *YES*___ *NO*___

    Do I live too much in the past? *YES*___ *NO*___

    Am I unrealistic about life in general? *YES*___ *NO*___

3. When a person is comfortable with himself, he has an easygoing attitude toward himself and others. He can laugh at himself. Now ask yourself:

    Am I often worried? *YES*___ *NO*___

    Do I take life too seriously? *YES*___ *NO*___

Am I stressed right now? *YES___ NO___*

Do I fail to laugh at myself often enough? *YES___ NO___*

Do I lack a sense of humor? *YES___ NO___*

Am I too tense in general? *YES___ NO___*

Am I still guilty of negative thinking at times? *YES___ NO___*

4. The person who feels comfortable with herself looks at herself "square in the eye" and knows herself well. Now ask yourself:

    Do I underestimate my ability and capacity? *YES___ NO___*

    Do I overestimate my ability and capacity? *YES___ NO___*

    Do I exaggerate my accomplishments? *YES___ NO___*

    Do I brag about myself? *YES___ NO___*

    Do I doubt my ability? *YES___ NO___*

    Do I fail to accept my limitations and shortcomings? *YES___ NO___*

    Am I making the most of my abilities? *YES___ NO___*

    Am I lax in my self-improvement program? *YES___ NO___*

    Am I failing to make the most of my opportunities? *YES___ NO___*

    Do I overindulge in sex? *YES___ NO___*

    Am I sexually frustrated? *YES___ NO___*

5. The person who is comfortable with himself has self-respect. Now ask yourself:

    Am I ashamed of myself for the work I do? *YES___ NO___*

    Am I ashamed of myself for the clothing I wear? *YES___ NO___*

    Am I ashamed of myself for living as I do? *YES___ NO___*

    Am I ashamed of myself for my personal appearance? *YES___ NO___*

    Am I ashamed of myself for my past behavior? *YES___ NO___*

    Am I carrying around guilt for my past mistakes? *YES___ NO___*

Am I ashamed of myself for what I should be doing but don't do? *YES___ NO__*

Am I ashamed of my personal habits? *YES___ NO___*

Am I ashamed of the company I keep? *YES___ NO___*

Do I feel that others do not respect me? *YES___ NO___*

6. A person who is comfortable with herself feels able to deal with most situations that come her way. Now ask yourself:

   Am I afraid of new places and new experiences? *YES___ NO___*

   Am I jittery and uncomfortable when I meet strangers? *YES___ NO___*

   Am I too shy? *YES___ NO___*

   Am I afraid to speak up when a store clerk makes a mistake? *YES___ NO___*

   Am I afraid to send food back in a restaurant? *YES___ NO___*

   Do I hesitate to call to the bus driver to stop the bus? *YES___ NO___*

   Am I unable to accept bad news gracefully and unemotionally? *YES___ NO__*

   Am I shy about speaking up for myself? *YES___ NO___*

   Am I timid in dealing with my boss? *YES___ NO___*

   Do I worry about things and "stew" in general? *YES___ NO___*

   Am I too high-strung and emotional in general? *YES___ NO___*

7. The person who is comfortable with himself gets satisfaction from simple everyday pleasures. Now ask yourself:

   Do I dislike staying at home? *YES___ NO___*

   Am I unhappy unless I am constantly "on the town?" *YES___ NO___*

   Am I lonely? *YES___ NO___*

   Do I need constant excitement to stay happy? *YES___ NO___*

   Is my life too complicated? *YES___ NO___*

   Is my life too boring? *YES___ NO___*

Do I complicate my life with extravagances I cannot afford? *YES___ NO___*

Am I dissatisfied with the life I am leading? *YES___ NO___*

Do I need more love in my personal life? *YES___ NO___*

Your answers to these questions pinpoint your troubles. Notice that each yes refers to an excess of some kind. This excess is a form of imbalance. Imbalance causes inner tension, stress, and strain. Thus, any yes you give reveals a source of your stress and strain.

Lesson 13
Current Self-Assessment

Some of us have experienced a wonderful increase in energy as the result of doing breathing exercises each morning and evening. Those of us who have been recording a daily inventory in our diaries have also been reaping the benefit of greater self-understanding and mental calmness. Each person who puts this entire program into action will enjoy renewed energy and physical and mental well-being.

First, we must stop ruining our health with tension and constriction, which come from negative thinking. We should be taking thought inventory every day (begun in assignment 1) to find out when and where we are negative, and we should be discontinuing such negativity, which robs us of needed energy. Second, after finishing a preliminary self-analysis, we will begin building energy and releasing tension through the breathing exercises and concentration exercises (begun in assignment 2). Third, we will develop mental power to accomplish our goals.

To analyze our negative thinking, in order to find the cause of our unpleasant emotions, we refer now to lesson 9 and the three formulas we need to follow to find health, happiness, and success:

1. To make a thing possible, we must first desire it.

2. What we desire, we must believe exists for us now.

3. The mind is like a magnet. It attracts what it is concentrating on.

These formulas are rooted in the Law of Belief. If you do not believe in yourself, you cannot succeed in anything. You must believe that you can succeed in this course of study and that these lessons will help you. Always remember: wholehearted efforts produce the best results in any endeavor.

If you know of other alcoholics struggling to be totally free from their disease, talk to them about your studies in this course. Just as we spoke constantly of alcoholism in the past, we must now speak constantly about the psychology of sobriety. We need to be around people who are engaged in the same process we are. Encourage others to proceed as you are doing. Carry the message of encouragement. Doing so helps create healthful emotions in you and in those around you.

Why must we talk about self-control and self-improvement rather than merely about the "good old drinking days"? Formula 3 tells us why. "The mind is like a magnet. It attracts what it is concentrating on." It is at this point that the average AA member falls behind those of us engaged in the active pursuit of real sobriety. We are no longer satisfied with superficial sobriety. We must now discipline our mind, analyze our thinking, and begin to lead an active, positive life, which will bring renewed health and happiness. We must think in terms of the three formulas and the Law of Belief and constantly discuss the psychology of sobriety with others who are similarly engaged. We need this kind of healthy "bull session" as encouragement and stimulation.

To sum up what we have said so far:

1. We must study and restudy the three formulas of daily thinking and make them a part of our daily life.

2. It is our duty and to our advantage to encourage those still only superficially sober to pursue real sobriety.

3. We need this companionship so we can discuss our progress and exchange opinions with others engaged in a similar pursuit.

If any of these methods struck a negative chord with you, this indicates you have an improper and negative attitude, although this may be deeply subconscious. For this reason, we will be completing the following self-inventory. It will help us discover the source of the negative emotions. No one will see this test but you, so be honest and answer as the person you actually are, not as the person you would like others to see you as.

YES NO
___ ___ Am I negative in my attitude right now?
___ ___ Have I neglected taking daily inventory?
___ ___ Am I under emotional strain?
___ ___ Am I "pushing" too hard?
___ ___ Am I forgetting to count my blessings?
___ ___ Is my old impatience returning?

___ ___ Do I expect too much too soon?
___ ___ Am I unwilling to discipline myself?
___ ___ Do I overlook my weaknesses?
___ ___ Am I failing to be honest with myself?
___ ___ Am I living in a fantasy?
___ ___ Do I lack energy?
___ ___ Do I have aches and pains?
___ ___ Do I lack the proper attitude toward life?
___ ___ Have I failed to do the breathing exercises?
___ ___ Do I lack the proper attitude toward my fellow humans?

If any of your answers are yes, you can be sure that the old alcoholic patterns of discouragement, resentment, self-pity, self-indulgence, and impatience are rearing their ugly heads. We strongly recommend that you have a stern talk with your misbehaving mind. Look into the mirror and say to yourself sternly, sharply, and loudly, in a most commanding voice:

> (Your name), stop feeling sorry for yourself! Stop that negative thinking and self-pity right now. Count your blessings and get busy on something constructive—*NOW*—and stop destroying yourself!

Always remember that we are no better than the condition of our minds. Neither money, nor friends, nor things alone can bring us happiness. They contribute to happiness only after we have acquired self-control. We must have self-control in order to get what we want. Without it, we are nothing. But self-control requires mind control, and mind control requires control of our senses. To understand our own self, we must know how our senses affect our mind and how our mind affects us, in right or wrong directions, according to how we use it. We must study ourselves, our habits, and our thinking. These lessons were formed to teach alcoholics the techniques of such self-study, because all drinking troubles come from an emotional immaturity that causes a lack of self-control.

These lessons teach us how to develop self-control and the power to concentrate through self-analysis. As a mere byproduct, our practices bring tranquility. The final result will be improved health and real serenity. Let us proceed now with our third self-analysis exercise.

Self-Knowledge Test 3

1. If your attitude is healthy, you are able to give love and to consider the interests of others.

    YES NO

    ___ ___ Do you try to run "roughshod" over other people?

    ___ ___ Do you sometimes fail to see the other fellow's point of view?

    ___ ___ Are you unable to show your affection to others?

    ___ ___ Do you dislike the opposite sex?

    ___ ___ Do you doubt the sincerity of other people?

    ___ ___ Do you resent certain people's mannerisms?

    ___ ___ Do "phonies" make you angry?

    ___ ___ Are you sometimes inconsiderate of others?

2. If your attitude is healthy, you will have personal relationships that are lasting and satisfying.

    YES NO

    ___ ___ Do you fail to have any long-standing friendships?

    ___ ___ Do you fail to take the initiative to make friends?

    ___ ___ Could you have "carried the message" better in AA?

    ___ ___ Are you helping someone struggling with alcoholism right now?

    ___ ___ Do you resent some AA members?

    ___ ___ Do you fail to have friends where you work?

    ___ ___ Do you have any violent dislikes?

    ___ ___ Do you wish you had a few good friends?

    ___ ___ Do you feel that this world is a "lousy place"?

    ___ ___ Do you feel that everyone is against you?

    ___ ___ Do you feel that everybody is out for himself?

3. If your attitude is healthy, you like others and trust others. You also take it for granted that others like and trust you.

   YES NO

   ___ ___ Do you have prejudices against people of other ethnicities or creeds?

   ___ ___ Do you feel that certain people justifiably don't like you?

   ___ ___ Are you afraid to trust certain people you know?

   ___ ___ Are you afraid that certain people are doing you harm?

   ___ ___ Are you afraid ahead of time that you won't like certain people?

   ___ ___ Are you hardheaded about certain ideas and situations?

   ___ ___ Would you be suspicious of you if you were somebody else?

   ___ ___ Do you consider yourself to be undependable?

   ___ ___ Do you consider yourself to be completely honest and trustworthy?

   ___ ___ Do you consider yourself to be superior in every way to other people?

4. If your attitude is healthy, you respect the many differences in other people.

   YES NO

   ___ ___ Do you criticize the habits and customs of people of other nationalities?

   ___ ___ Do you look down on people of other ethnicities or creeds?

   ___ ___ Are you intolerant of people with accents or speech defects?

   ___ ___ Are you what some people might call a "snob"?

5. If your attitude is healthy, you do not push people around. Neither do you allow yourself to be pushed around.

   YES NO

   ___ ___ Do you take advantage of those under your direction?

   ___ ___ Do you feel superior to people of other ethnicities or creeds?

   ___ ___ Do you feel inferior to others who have more money and power?

   ___ ___ Do you ever let yourself be intimidated by your boss?

___ ___ Are you unduly impressed by wealth, power, or social position?

___ ___ Do you often fail to stand up for your rights?

___ ___ Are you the "Casper Milquetoast" or wishy-washy type?

___ ___ Are you afraid to speak up at the time a thing happens?

___ ___ Or do you complain after the thing is all over?

___ ___ Does anyone or anything have you intimidated at this very moment?

___ ___ Do you have anyone under your power at this moment?

6. If your attitude is healthy, you can feel that you are part of a group.

    YES NO

    ___ ___ Do you feel as if you belong to nobody and nothing?

    ___ ___ Do you feel like an outcast, without friends or loyalties?

    ___ ___ Do you feel like a misfit?

    ___ ___ Do you lack the proper enthusiasm to follow through with these lessons?

    ___ ___ Have you failed to find and help another alcoholic who could benefit from these lessons?

    ___ ___ Are you insincere about carrying this message and helping others?

    ___ ___ Are you failing to look around for another alcoholic to help?

7. If your attitude is healthy, you feel a sense of responsibility to your neighbors and to every living being.

    YES NO

    ___ ___ Do you resent the rest of the world?

    ___ ___ Do you feel that you have had a "rough deal"?

    ___ ___ Do you feel that others are responsible for you?

    ___ ___ Do you think the world owes you something?

    ___ ___ Are you failing to pay your own way?

_____ _____ Are you ever guilty of being untruthful toward others?

_____ _____ Do you fail to have a "spirit of brotherhood" attitude?

_____ _____ Do you feel that everybody is completely selfish?

_____ _____ Do you fail sometimes to practice the golden rule?

If you have read each question carefully and answered to the best of your knowledge, your answers reflect your true feelings. Your yes answers reveal your trouble spots. Bear in mind that these are mental immaturities that cause you pain, tension, and constriction. You must correct these negative attitudes. Then you will see and feel your health improve, and see and feel others' attitudes toward you change. Then you will be surer of yourself in all situations.

Find all of your yes answers and ask yourself: Why do I feel this way or act this way? By finding the why behind each source of trouble, you will discover why you are not completely happy with yourself.

Finding the why is the first job. Learning the right action is the next job. Taking the right action is the final job. We are still searching for the trouble spots.

Lesson 14
Finding the Roots of Unhappiness

Happiness is the absence of pain. This is a simple sentence, but it contains the wisdom of the ages. It applies to no one better than to the alcoholic.

The alcoholic drinks to escape physical or mental pain, whether he knows it or not. Alcohol is his crutch. He uses it to bolster his ego in order to face situations he cannot face sober. He uses it to blot out certain memories he cannot face. He uses it to build up a life of fantasy because he does not feel comfortable in his own life. He uses it because he does not know how to adjust to life without the crutch of a drink. A happy person needs no such crutch.

If happiness is the absence of pain, the process of finding happiness is the process of freeing ourselves from those things that cause us pain. But the peculiarity of the mind is to escape unhappiness. The mind takes every way out of its unhappiness except to face the source of the unhappiness. This is the difference between a strong person and a weak person: The strong person has control over her mind; the weak person, due to various mental immaturities, does not. All alcoholics have such mental immaturities to varying degrees. Until they do away with them, they are always a potential "sucker" for that first drink.

This is a difficult point to get across to most alcoholics, who are so distracted that they are unable to look into themselves. They are not to be blamed for not seeing the truth; they are simply not ready for this phase of their recovery, just as some drinking alcoholics are not yet ready for AA. These lessons are for the alcoholic who is both ready and able to look within for past and present troubles. This alcoholic knows that happiness is an "inside job."

One way people try to end unhappiness is to substitute one thing for another thing, such as substituting one type of food for another when a person is on a diet. The other way is to substitute right ideas that will calm the mind. Doing this, we gain the chance to then use self-analysis to find the cause of our unhappiness. Much of the world goes along thinking wrongly that the only way to happiness is to acquire more and more possessions. This philosophy of life, materialism, is clearly not the answer. In our very materialistic country, there are an ever-growing number of mentally ill individuals and alcoholics.

The alcoholic uses alcohol to anesthetize his painful emotions. The drug addict and the rank materialist do the same sort of thing, each trying to escape unhappiness in his own way. But true escape comes only from within, through peace of mind. Does not the Bible tell us to seek the kingdom of heaven within? This is just another way to point out the necessity of self-analysis.

Do not misunderstand the intent here. People must work, must have things, must enjoy their lives—but in moderation. In finding the sources of our pain, we must find out where we are not being moderate in our demands upon ourselves and others. We must seek balance. Otherwise, we will be striving too hard or not hard enough. Either way, we will be robbed of needed energy, which is the source of all mind power.

The only way to find true happiness is to seek the cause of our present unhappiness. We must get at the roots of our dissatisfaction with life. When we find this, we must take action in a balanced, realistic manner to change our lives and replace unwanted conditions with those we desire. The basis of life is growth and improvement. If we are to improve, we must improve our mind, for the mind is the basis of all thought, and thought is the basis for all action that creates things and conditions.

In concluding our preliminary self-analysis, we will examine our ability to meet the demands of life. Again, we need to meet three conditions to be completely well-adjusted:

1. We must feel comfortable about ourselves.

2. We must feel right about other people.

3. We must be able to meet the demands of life.

Lacking any of these, we cannot have health, happiness, and success.

Self-Knowledge Test 4

1. If your attitude is healthy, you are able to meet the demands of life by doing something about problems *as they arise.*

    YES NO

    ___ ___ Do you procrastinate?

    ___ ___ Do you shrink away from doing unpleasant tasks?

___ ___ Are you failing to apply the lessons presented in this book?

___ ___ Are you worrying right now about unsolved problems?

___ ___ Are you failing to take action to solve problems?

___ ___ Is your life, at this moment, too much for you?

___ ___ Are you failing to do your utmost in every area?

2. If your attitude is healthy, you set realistic goals for yourself to meet the demands of life.

    YES NO

    ___ ___ Do you "bite off more than you can chew"?

    ___ ___ Are you always behind schedule?

    ___ ___ Are you under stress and strain?

    ___ ___ Do you overestimate your ability to produce?

    ___ ___ Are you living in a fantasy?

    ___ ___ Do you follow get-rich-quick schemes?

    ___ ___ Do you daydream about your future?

    ___ ___ Do you fail to make a daily plan of action?

    ___ ___ Are you drifting right now?

    ___ ___ Do you lack a goal in life?

3. If you are able to meet the demands of life, you are able to think for yourself and make your own decisions and stick to them.

    YES NO

    ___ ___ Do you always seek advice before taking action?

    ___ ___ Are you generally unsure of yourself?

    ___ ___ Are you often indecisive?

    ___ ___ Are you confused about anything right now?

    ___ ___ Is it hard for you to make decisions?

4. If you are able to meet the demands of life, you always put your best effort into what you do, and you get great satisfaction out of it.

   YES NO

   ___ ___ Do you dislike your job?

   ___ ___ Do you work just to get by?

   ___ ___ Do you fail to give your best to your job?

   ___ ___ Do you lack a long-term desire for the future?

   ___ ___ Are you lacking in enthusiasm these days?

   ___ ___ Do you dislike your employers?

   ___ ___ Are you a "floater"?

5. If you are able to meet the demands of life, you are thoroughly optimistic, happy, enthusiastic, and energetic. You also have a definite plan for the present and future.

   YES NO

   ___ ___ Do you lack energy?

   ___ ___ Are you lethargic?

   ___ ___ Are you unhappy?

   ___ ___ Do you lack enthusiasm?

   ___ ___ Are you often negative?

   ___ ___ Are you a hypochondriac?

   ___ ___ Do you often talk about your troubles?

   ___ ___ Are you a constant complainer?

   ___ ___ Do you lack a definite plan for tomorrow?

   ___ ___ Do you lack a definite plan for the weekend?

   ___ ___ Do you lack a life plan?

   ___ ___ Are you failing to do your utmost with your self-analysis?

   ___ ___ Do you fear the future?

___ ___ Do you fear death?

___ ___ Do you live with a terrible sense of foreboding?

Every yes answer shows where you are out of balance. If you reread each yes response, you will discover that behind each answer is some kind of negative attitude.

If you cannot honestly figure out why you are lacking in certain things at present and why you feel the way you do, then you need to boost your self-knowledge. Here are actions to take if you are "stuck":

(1) Follow the eleventh Step of AA and meditate. Through meditation the Higher Power can bring serenity and enable us to overcome our psychological problems. The breathing exercises and concentration exercises (explained in assignment 2) release tensions and help a person begin to meditate. In meditation we turn our mind to the Higher Power and concentrate on it. There are different methods for meditation practice, such as visualizing one's concept of a Higher Power or repeating Bible verses or spiritual sayings of one's faith. The aim is to turn our mind away from the material world and concentrate on the Higher Power, the unseen power.

(2) Continue to study these lessons.

(3) Continue to do self-analysis and seek honest conclusions, and then take action to improve your reactions to persons, places, and things. Self-understanding will come.

Lesson 15
The Basis of All Negative Emotions

We have discovered that each of our problems falls into one of three areas:

1. Our feelings about ourselves.

2. Our feelings about other people.

3. Our feelings about conditions, places, and things.

We have learned that if we are happy with ourselves, our emotions will be pleasant and we will feel at peace toward other people. We will be able to meet the demands of life.

Without exception, every one of us has fallen down in one or more of these categories. Our yes answers in the self-knowledge tests reveal where we are out of balance. By studying these areas, we will gradually be able to understand the reasons we are out of balance.

In order to advance further in health, happiness, and success, we must continue to change any remaining alcoholic thinking to the right kind of thinking. We must know what this right kind of thinking is and understand why it works. Then we must learn the technique of applying this right thinking to every area of our life.

While pleasant emotions create health, unpleasant emotions create tensions and constrictions that can lead to serious illness. We must find out where we are negative and out of balance, and then correct the negativity and keep it under control. Doing this will require us to develop willpower and mind control. Willpower and mind control give us the strength to correct weaknesses, build health, and develop the stamina and fortitude we need to attain our goals in life. If we follow through with each step in these lessons, we will succeed.

In lesson 6, we read how Dr. Penfield proved that various parts of the brain store different past experiences. It is a fact that we have a subconscious or unconscious mind that stores memories of happy and unhappy events. Our memories are part of our brain, and our unpleasant emotions are still with us and still affecting our body and mind in an adverse way. We must rid ourselves of these unpleasant emotions. How do we do this? First, we must understand how we began to experience these unpleasant emotions.

As explained earlier, every thought we think registers upon our mind with a corresponding emotion. It is our unpleasant thoughts that create unpleasant emotions; and it is our unpleasant emotions that create tensions and constrictions that adversely affect our glands, nerves, and muscles. This is the basis of all psychosomatic illness. For example, suppose an elderly parent continues to correct an adult child to the point of embarrassing the adult child in front of others. The adult child, no doubt, dislikes this treatment (has unpleasant thoughts) and feels unpleasant emotions. Feelings of anger, shame, and anxiety can create tensions and constrictions of muscles that result in overstimulation of glands producing hormonal imbalance: the result may be psychosomatic illnesses manifesting in such ways as "unexplainable" headaches, abdominal spasms, high blood pressure, etc.

But, we might ask, what causes unpleasant emotions? The answer is *fear*. Fear is behind all unpleasant emotions, whether we know it or not. Some fears are deeply imbedded, not apparent until we trace them to their source. In these lessons, we analyze ourselves to find our negative reactions; all negative reactions are rooted in fear. Once we know where we are negative, we must find out why. Then we will be able to remove our long-standing, hidden fears from our subconscious mind, the storehouse of memories. There is a definite science to doing this.

Every drinking alcoholic is a maladjusted individual. The degree of his recovery, after he stops drinking, will be proportional to the degree he removes his maladjustment though self-understanding. The state of real sobriety is the state of complete self-understanding. In this state we are healthy and happy. The more we study our feelings by tracing the thoughts and motives which are behind these feelings, the more we progress to the state of true sobriety. For example, suppose John finds himself wanting a drink each night after work. There could be many reasons for this. Perhaps John feels dominated by his boss and suppresses his anger all day long; he finds release from this suppressed anger by drinking. Or suppose John does not want to face his wife and children for some reason. Thus, he stops off at the bar to procrastinate going home and listening to a complaining wife and unruly children. In both cases, John's drinking comes from his inability to deal with problems he does not want to face. Why? He fears taking corrective action. Why? He lacks the courage to do this. Why? John has to seek this answer, and keep seeking answers to develop self-understanding. This is how self-study proceeds: asking the "why" and seeking the answer. John's continual study of himself, his motives, his fears, and his wishes, will bring him the answers he needs to change unwanted behavior. The daily self-inventory could become a part of every person's life, alcoholic or not, to develop self-understanding and better adjustment to life.

Worry and anxiety are manifestations of fear. Is a happy person fearful? Certainly not. Is a fearful person happy? Again, certainly not. Fear and happiness are at completely opposite poles. Fear brings pain; happiness is an absence of pain. And how do both manifest themselves? In other words, how do we recognize a fearful person, or a happy one? By looking at his face, by noticing his mannerisms, by listening to his voice, and so on. The telltale reactions to fear and happiness are noticeable to the discerning eye.

We cannot hide our emotions. Every thought has an accompanying emotion. Not even the best poker player alive can stop his body from reacting to his thoughts. Our bodies mirror the condition of our minds. What links thought to emotion or mind to body is the autonomic nervous system. We either think fearful thoughts or happy thoughts, and their effects become manifest in our body.

"But," we might protest in reading this, "sometimes we have no control over our emotions." This is true, but we are going to gain such control. This is what we call self-control. It comes in direct proportion to our control over our mind. And control over our mind comes only after we understand our mind. To do this, we must become familiar with the term *psychoneuroses*.

A drinking alcoholic is a psychoneurotic. *Psycho* refers to the mind; *neurotic* describes a highly nervous condition. A drinking alcoholic is a person who is in a highly nervous state of mind. How did he get that way? He got that way by entertaining thoughts of anxiety and worry, which are manifestations of fear. "Fear of what?" we might ask. Fear of anything under the sun—justified fears and unjustified fears, fears based upon reality and upon unreality. But how do these fears begin?

Our alcoholic fears arose because we conditioned ourselves to be in a constant state of anxiety or worry. By the time the alcoholic drinks to escape tension (known or unknown), he has put his body under continual stress, which has resulted in overstimulation of the endocrine gland. In an actual emergency, the gland's excess production of hormones is temporary. But the alcoholic's constant anxiety places his body under a perpetual "emergency call," overstimulating his endocrine glands and doing great harm to his body.

Perhaps we suffered fear because we became stuck in a situation with no solution. Not being able to face our problems and escape the unpleasant circumstances, we were fearful. We drank to ease the pain.

Regardless of what negative action we took while drinking, such as yelling or disappearing for several days, etc., we must realize that we were not responsible. We were sick, or psychoneurotic. In our highly nervous state of worry and anxiety, we did what we thought was right. For most of us, this anxiety was deeply subconscious, rooted in our conditioning from childhood to think fearful thoughts. This conditioning made us introverted or insecure, or anxious or worried or unsure of ourselves in general, and it became difficult for us to adjust properly to life. As these unpleasant and painful emotions became more and more a part of us, life became harder and harder to cope with. Eventually we took to alcoholic drinking, either to ease the tension of painful situations or to escape ourselves entirely.

If the conditioning of our thoughts toward worry and anxiety began in early childhood, we were like the sheep, described earlier, that was conditioned to fear to the point of near death. We escaped anxiety by anesthetizing our minds with alcohol. If you look around, you will see people who are not alcoholics but who are still suffering the tension and constriction caused by fear. Some people use drugs to escape pain; some people overeat when they are upset; some people shop or go to the store to seek "pleasantness" by acquiring more material things. Alcoholics drink because of psychoneurotic fear (whether they realize it or not), but alcoholism is merely one kind of adjustment to psychoneuroses.

We must uncover our fears. They are based upon our present and past anxieties, which, in turn, come from our feelings of insecurity, inadequacy, and the like. Working backward, we must trace any present feelings of worry and anxiety. Until we do this, we will be the victims of pain and unhappiness and, possibly, of severe illness. The dangerous chain reaction of unpleasant emotions is shown in the following diagram.

THE VICIOUS CIRCLE OF UNPLEASANT EMOTIONS

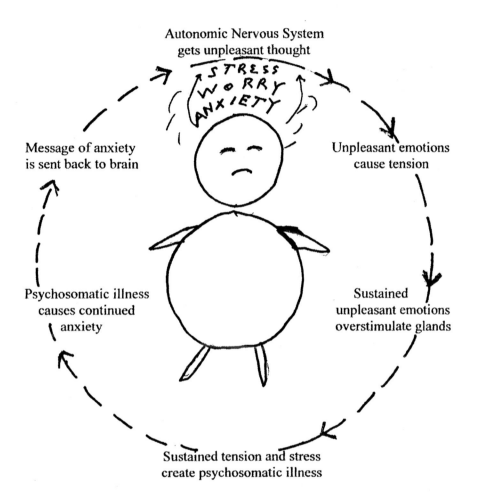

Autonomic Nervous System
gets unpleasant thought

Message of anxiety
is sent back to brain

Unpleasant emotions
cause tension

Psychosomatic illness
causes continued
anxiety

Sustained
unpleasant emotions
overstimulate glands

Sustained tension and stress
create psychosomatic illness

Lesson 16
The Improvement of Mental and Physical Health

We mentioned that our job would be threefold. We need to:

1. Find out what is wrong with our lives, what we want to change, and why we are not happy.

2. Improve our mental and physical health.

3. Move forward to attain our desired goals.

We should now be ready for the second step, the improvement of our mental and physical health. But we should check ourselves. Do we understand everything presented so far? Are we taking daily inventory of our negative emotions? Are we performing the daily breathing exercises? Are we using the three formulas of daily thinking? Are we rereading these lessons over and over again? If we answer no to any of these questions, we are not doing ourselves justice.

We have read that any alcoholic with the interest, energy, and sobriety needed to understand and apply these teachings can vastly improve her mental and physical health. She can develop new self-understanding and get a new slant on alcoholism as it applies to her individually. She can develop a philosophy of life that will bring new consciousness and independence. She can develop the mind power and personal magnetism she's always wanted. She can develop the qualities of dependability, calmness, and self-command. This list of possible achievements is not mere words, not idle promises. It contains statements of fact based upon scientific principles. It describes the accomplishments of other alcoholics who studied these principles and applied them successfully to their lives.

To read these lessons is not enough. Reading alone will not make our goals come true. These lessons involve a real program of action. We are aiming to achieve something else now besides the condition of merely not taking a drink.

Not only are we going to stay sober, we are going to lose our very appetite for alcohol and understand why. Besides this, we are going to attain calmness, self-control, and unending physical and mental energy. We are going to end depressions, dry drunks, and "pink cloud" giddiness. How? We are going to develop real sobriety.

Let us review some major points:

1. Every time we think an unpleasant thought, we are creating unpleasant emotions. These unpleasant emotions start a cause-and-effect chain reaction that robs us of needed energy, damages our health, and disturbs our mind.

2. The results of our self-analysis tests tell us where we are failing in our jobs and in our relationships with people, and why we are not satisfied with ourselves.

3. We should know the three formulas of daily thinking and believe in them:

    • To make a thing possible, we must first desire it.

    • What we desire, we must believe exists for us now.

    • The mind is like a magnet. It attracts what it is concentrating on.

4. We are the sum total of our past thoughts. Every one of our past experiences is indelibly impressed upon our subconscious mind, and will remain there until it is released. Meditation will release these unpleasant emotions. Meanwhile, we must prevent their reappearance by thinking positively and keeping ourselves in a constant state of pleasant emotions. We can accomplish this through continuous practice.

5. Now, what should we be doing?

    • We should be taking daily inventory and recording our negative emotions in our diaries. We can refer to the diaries to study ourselves honestly and fearlessly. We should have a sincere desire to understand ourselves and learn why we think wrong things. We should have a sincere desire to do the right thing and know truth.

    • We should be optimistic and seek constant self-improvement. We should believe with all our hearts that a life of health and happiness awaits us, for it truly does if we proceed to make it possible.

    • We should be ready to go into action to improve our health. This means taking 30 to 45 minutes a day, partly in the morning and partly in the evening if desired, to learn how to relax from the tensions that still remain with us.

- We should learn more about the operation of the body and how the disease of alcoholism affects nerves and glands.

- We should retake the self-analysis tests periodically to assess our progress.

Now we must build up energy. Unfortunately, the bodies of most alcoholics have been torn down through years of drinking, and they never fully recuperate to become as strong as they once were. But we are going to combine self-analysis with mental and physical improvement and develop energy we never had before.

Listed below are some specific guidelines for starting the recovery process.

1. Set a goal for yourself, something like, "Today I will carry a small notebook and write down instances of negative feelings, and I will study these negative feelings in the evening."

2. Tackle a goal each day, something that you feel you *can* do. For instance, promise yourself that you will respond in a pleasant manner all morning. The next day, tackle being pleasant all afternoon. On the third day, affirm that you will respond pleasantly all day long.

3. Keep your anxiety level as low as possible. "Be still."

4. Keep quiet about your past activities: change your life and start over.

5. Make a geographical change, temporarily, to keep old pain associations from being reawakened. Stay away from places of unhappiness until you achieve detachment. For example, find a different route to work instead of traversing the same old roads. Avoid all streets where bars exist. Take a weekend vacation to another town or campsite. Go to a new restaurant. Visit a museum in your city. Take a walk in the park. The list of new activities is endless.

6. Meditate daily.

7. Try to establish regular habits. For example, have a definite rising time each day (sleep later on days off from work, if needed). Have three meals a day, even if some are light meals. Set a time for regular exercise several times a week. Make it a habit to learn the local, national, and international news to develop interests beyond ourselves. Include time for your hobby (gardening, carpentry, sewing, reading, etc.) Make your daily inventory and daily medi-

tation a priority. Set a time for turning off the TV at night and getting enough sleep at night.

8. Don't dwell on your failures. Should you fail in attaining a goal, start over with renewed faith and calm determination. Moreover, turn the failure into a marvelous opportunity to study what went wrong and learn by it.

9. Continue to take daily inventory, making it a priority in your schedule.

10. Continue to practice relaxation and breathing exercises. Observe how much more relaxed you feel following these exercises.

The questions you must ask are: "Am I really sincere about improving my heath, and am I ready to give 30 to 45 minutes a day to this? Am I ready to discipline myself to carry on this program at home on my own?"

From here on, this plan for self-improvement is in your hands. We hope you see it though.

Glossary

These terms are used in Alcoholics Anonymous.

Higher Power: The belief in a Power greater than oneself; the concept that a Higher Power exists and is open to all people; one's personal concept of God, called the Higher Power and existing for everyone.

The *Twelve Steps* of Alcoholics Anonymous:

1. We admitted we were powerless over alcohol—that our lives had become unmanageable.

2. We came to believe that a Power greater than ourselves could restore us to sanity.

3. We made a decision to turn our will and our lives over to the care of God *as we understood Him.*

4. We made a searching and fearless moral inventory of ourselves.

5. We admitted to God, to ourselves, and to another human being the exact nature of our wrongs.

6. We were entirely ready to have God remove all these defects of character.

7. We humbly asked Him to remove our shortcomings.

8. We made a list of all persons we had harmed, and became willing to make amends to them all.

9. We made direct amends to such people wherever possible, except when to do so would injure them or others.

10. We continued to take personal inventory and when we were wrong promptly admitted it.

11. We sought through prayer and meditation to improve our conscious contact with God *as we understood Him,* praying only for knowledge of His will for us and the power to carry that out.

12. Having had a spiritual awakening as the result of these steps, we tried to carry this message to alcoholics, and to practice these principles in all our affairs.

From *Alcoholics Anonymous,* 3rd edition. New York: Alcoholics Anonymous World Services, Inc., 1976, p. 59–60.

Selected Bibliography

Alcoholics Anonymous. 3rd ed. New York: Alcoholics Anonymous World Services Inc., 1976.

Felitti, Vincent J. "Caring for Patients." Review of *Caring for People,* by Allen Barbour. The Permanente Journal, Fall 1997, http://xnet.kp.org/permanentejournal/fall97pj/caring.html.

Schindler, John A. *How to Live 365 Days a Year.* New York: Fawcett Crest Books, 1954.

Twelve Steps and Twelve Traditions. New York: Alcoholics Anonymous World Services Inc., 1988.

978-0-595-36095-6
0-595-36095-5

Printed in the United Kingdom
by Lightning Source UK Ltd.
109169UKS00002B/94-108